Of Men and Mary is superb. The six life testi[...] miraculous, heroic, and truly inspiring. They illustrate the reality of divine grace of Jesus through Mary and the triumph of the human will for good over evil, light over darkness. *Of Men and Mary* is an injection of hope in a historical time when it is so essential to spiritually thrive.

Fr. Gary Thomas
Pastor, exorcist, and subject of the book and movie, "The Rite."

I was deeply moved by this beautiful book. There is an anointing upon it: the Spirit of God radiates through its words. As I read the stories therein, I felt myself touched by grace, by a desire for deeper conversion, and I kept thinking about the words from the Book of Revelation: "They defeated him [the devil] by the blood of the Lamb and the word of their testimony" (Rev. 12:11). Being someone whose life was changed because of a book—*Medjugorje: The Message*—as a senior in college, I know how important and powerful a spiritually impactful book can be. This book, I feel, has that same ability to transform lives, to free people from darkness. *Of Men and Mary* is raw, vulnerable, deeply edifying, and inspiring. It is the kind of book you will want to give out to people, especially those in need of hope. I plan to share this tremendous work with many through the years.

Br. Daniel Maria Klimek, T.O.R.
Assistant Professor, Theology Department
Franciscan University of Steubenville, Ohio

St. Ephrem the Syrian, a priest and poet from the 4th century, taught that the Virgin Mary is a "ship of treasures" for all who take refuge in her. *Of Men and Mary* presents the awe-inspiring stories of six men whose lives were changed—and manhood healed—when they entrusted their lives to Mary, the ship of treasures. This book is anointed!"

Fr. Donald Calloway, MIC
Author of *No Turning Back: A Witness to Mercy* and
Marian Gems: Daily Wisdom on Our Lady

I love this book! It contains clear and touching examples of how heaven is closer to us than we are to ourselves, of how Mary is the Good Mother who keeps *all* of us in her heart. To read *Of Men and Mary* is to step into the graces of Medjugorje, a place that brought heaven very close to me. There I felt so much joy and so loved by God that I would often cry. There

i

I could smell and feel holiness. During my first pilgrimage, I noticed I could stare directly at the sun for the entire week and for as long as I liked. Mary is in Medjugorje, I have no doubt. I saw, I felt, I know, and no one can ever take that away from me. Through these stories, the same Mary who reached out to me is ready to come close to you and fill you with love. *"If you knew how much I love you,"* she says in Medjugorje, *"you would cry for joy."*

Fr. Bernardin Mugabo
Pastor of St. John the Evangelist Church, Carmichael, California

Of Men and Mary is a fantastic treasure trove of the life experiences of six men who bravely bare their souls and secrets. Their courage and trust in Mary while traveling unknown, winding roads is astounding and profoundly moving. This life-changing book made me laugh and cry from the start. I recommend it to all men, as it will deepen their faith and devotion to Christ and His mother. I also recommend it to all women, as these men will touch their hearts with the unique challenges they face. Women will want the men in their lives to read it—fathers, husbands, and sons—but it will help *anyone* wanting a deeper connection with Jesus and the Blessed Mother. Reading it reminded me of the miracles I experienced in Medjugorje and the active role Mary has played in my life. This memorable book has given me a spiritual "shot in the arm" and a resurgence of love for Our Lady, Queen of Peace, and the messages of Medjugorje. A must-read for all!

Gretchen Harris
Catholic Recording Artist

As our world darkens, the love of God, made manifest in the details of these six testimonies, astonishes us! We need to be astonished! God really does love us, and Our Lady's presence in Medjugorje and in these men's lives is an expression of His great love in our troubled times. I thank each witness who has shared with us the story of his rescue, and God bless Christine Watkins for expressing them so artfully. Indeed, Our Lady thanks you, as well: *"You, who live in the love of God and have experienced His gifts, witness them with your words and life that they may be for the joy and encouragement to others."* This book is a great work of mercy—may many of God's children find hope and encouragement through its true stories!

Denis Nolan
MaryTV.tv

When we open our hearts to the power of Medjugorje, we see that there is a need for change, a need for peace. Christine Watkins' book proves that peace is possible in the world because it is possible in our own personal lives. Our Lady says, *"Dear children, may today be the day when you place God at the first place in your lives, may today be the day when you start loving!"* It is only through love and prayer that we find the filler for that gap, that aching hole and emptiness in our lives, especially in today's world. This book is a treasure. It perfectly relays Our Lady's messages in Medjugorje without preaching. May all those who read it be blessed and changed by the testimonies within its covers.

Sr. Emmanuel Maillard
Author of nine books, including
Scandalous Mercy: When God Goes Beyond Boundaries

Of Men and Mary is most uplifting and inspirational. Like St. Ignatius of Loyola, who was always on the verge of holy tears because of his sensitivity to God's blessings, I found myself in tears, reading how God, the "Hound of Heaven," pursued these souls, never giving up on them. This book is filled with exactly what the world so desperately needs: extraordinary hope. I found myself craving more. . . perhaps a sequel?

June Klins
Author of *I Have Come to Tell the World That God Exists*
Editor of *The Spirit of Medjugorje* monthly newsletter

Watch the book trailer for
Of Men and Mary by going to
www.queenofpeacemedia.com/men
and see the faces of the men whose
stories grace this book:

a convicted murder
a lamb who lost everything
a man caught in illicit sexual relationships
a football player tackled by the Blessed Mother
a married man whose marriage was as good as dead
and a man who literally died and came back to life

Explore our Catholic media:
books, videos, blogs, prayer
requests, and more, that help
you nurture your faith and
"Find your way Home."
Go to:
www.QueenofPeaceMedia.com.

Also Visit Us on Social Media!
SUBSCRIBE, LIKE, AND FOLLOW US!

At www.YouTube.com, search for Queen of Peace Media
Facebook: www.facebook.com/QueenofPeaceMedia
Pinterest: www.pinterest.com/catholicvideos
Instagram: www.instagram.com/QueenofPeaceMedia

RADIO MARIA SHOW
"Find Something More, Find Your Way Home"
with Kendra and Christine

Tune into Christine Watkins' live weekly show with Kendra Von Esh, Thursdays at 7 p.m. to 8 p.m., P.S.T., also posted on Queen of Peace Media's YouTube channel. To watch or be notified of our new YouTube videos, see http://bit.ly/2HDl65U and click "Subscribe" and the bell icon (top right of the screen). Also go to www.queenofpeacemedia.com/home.

Christine Watkins (www.ChristineWatkins.com) is an inspirational Catholic speaker and author. Her books include the Catholic best-seller, *Full of Grace: Miraculous Stories of Healing and Conversion through Mary's Intercession; Mary's Mantle Consecration: A Spiritual Retreat for Heaven's Help; Transfigured: Patricia Sandoval's Escape from Drugs, Homelessness, and the Back Doors of Planned Parenthood*—available in English and Spanish; and *The Warning: Testimonies and Prophecies of the Illumination of Conscience*. For details, see the end of this book.

Formerly an anti-Christian atheist living a life of sin, Watkins began a life of service to the Catholic Church after a miraculous healing from Jesus through Mary, which saved her from death. Her story can be found in the book, *Full of Grace*. Before her conversion, Watkins danced professionally with the San Francisco Ballet Company. Today, she has twenty years of experience as a keynote speaker, retreat leader, spiritual director, and counselor—with ten years working as a hospice grief counselor and another ten as a post-abortion healing director. Christine Watkins lives in Sacramento, California with her husband and two sons.

OF MEN AND MARY

How Six Men Won the Greatest Battle of Their Lives

Christine Watkins

ISBN-13: 978-1-947701-04-5
ISBN-10: 1-947701-04-5

CONTENTS

FOREWORD

I am not a convert but what is considered a "revert" to the faith: someone who grew up Catholic but strayed from Catholicism, only to discover years later that his home was in the Church he'd left fourteen years before.

When I came back to the Church after my "Prodigal Son" wanderings through stand-up comedy, girlfriends, unfulfilling jobs, and a stint with a rock band, I became reacquainted with the Rosary. Initially, I didn't want to make this prayer a part of my life because I found it needlessly repetitious and solidly boring, but then I knew no prayer devotion other than this. (In my preteen years, my Austrian grandmother had me saying all fifteen decades.) Although it was a real struggle to begin again, the Rosary gave me a better understanding of Mary in her role as not only the mother of Jesus, but especially as my mother. I also imagined my role as a son of Mary. Without knowing why, this made sense to me.

I recall speaking to my dad one evening, a short time after my return to the Church, asking him questions about Our Lady in Holy Scripture. He began to explain the importance of Mary's Fiat to God and her role in Jesus' first miracle. He then asked me if I had heard of a place that started with an "M." I asked, "Where's that?"

He replied, "It's in old Yugoslavia." My only understanding of old Yugoslavia was that a bitter war was happening on their soil, and it didn't look like it was going to end soon. My father then asked, "Did you know that Our Lady is appearing there?" I stopped and stared at him as if this were impossible, and still, I wanted nothing more than to learn about this supposed apparition. He gave me the book, *Medjugorje: The Message* by Wayne Weible. I took it home, thinking, "I have no idea if this is real, but I am willing to give it a read."

I am not a quick reader. It takes me at least a couple of weeks to get through a book. Of course, there are mitigating factors: I tend to make too many commitments. However, when I pored over this account of the apparitions at Medjugorje, I was engrossed until the early hours of the morning. Every chapter was so fascinating that I couldn't imagine reading about anything else. Two days before, I had never heard about this tiny village half way around the world in Bosnia-Herzegovina, and now I desired to be there.

As soon as I left work the day after completing the first book, I bought the second one, *Medjugorje: The Mission*. I wanted to talk to the visionaries, to anyone involved. If I met a former Medjugorje pilgrim, I had to soak up every word of their account of this faraway, middle-of-nowhere place. I needed to listen to priests who had traveled there on pilgrimage. If there was a Medjugorje conference, I had to go to it.

But above all, I had to live the primary messages that Our Lady was giving us through the six visionaries who were seeing Mary face-to-face: attend Holy Mass; pray the Rosary; go to Confession; read the Bible; and fast twice a week. The last of these five, fasting, was, and still is, challenging to me; but as I understand it, if it were easy, where is the sacrifice?

Within three months after I began living Mary's requests, I saw a difference in how I perceived my life. I no longer desired to go out on Fridays and Saturdays. I was no longer watching TV, as if that were my only option. I was making choices that were life- and faith-affirming. Living the messages of Medjugorje led me right to Jesus and into the priesthood. I answered the call in the spring of 1995 and entered the seminary in the fall of 1996. In 2005, I was ordained for the Archdiocese of Los Angeles, California.

I am fascinated by accounts of individuals who made an honest discovery about Jesus and His Church, and who like myself, made "the journey home." I also know firsthand how a book can change one's life. *Of Men and Mary* has this great potential. Author and speaker, Christine Watkins, has inspired many with her first book, *Full of Grace: Miraculous Stories of Healing and Conversion through Mary's Intercession*. *Of Men and Mary* will no doubt do the same. Amazing are the challenges encountered by Fr. Rick Wendell and Fr. Michael Lightner. Incredible are the stories of the Leatherby family and the complicated life of Chris Watkins. Shocking are the sudden turns in the journeys of Fr. Paul Caporali and Jim Jennings. Even when all of the problematic circumstances surrounding each individual seem insurmountable, God makes a way for the soul to find its way back to Jesus through His Blessed Mother. Every one of these accounts is well written and brings to life the truth of the archangel Gabriel's message to Mary: "Nothing is impossible for God" (Luke 1:37). It is my hope that through *Of Men and Mary*, you will allow yourself or someone close to you to make this same beautiful discovery.

Fr. Bob Garon
Pastor of St. Didacus Church
Los Angeles, California

INTRODUCTION

Turn these pages, and you will find yourself surprisingly inspired by a murderer locked up in prison, a drug-using football player who dreamed of the pros, and a selfish, womanizing dare-devil who died and met God— and lived again. You will root for a husband and father whose marriage was a battleground, a man pulled by lust and illicit attractions, searching desperately to belong, and an innocent lamb who lost, in a single moment, everyone he cared about most. And you will rejoice that their sins and their pasts were no obstacle for heaven. These men became living beacons of hope, walking proof of human triumph over spiritual darkness.

In the heat of the fiercest of spiritual battles, when all seemed lost and these men were left with nothing to stand on but stormy seas, they were given a lifeboat, a new path in life—one that they never dreamed of, not for an instant. They were pulled in a different direction that, at first, they didn't want, and then at last, they loved. In the boat of safety, they sailed with sure victory into breathtaking, unknown vistas. Some became priests—one, a deacon, and two have since reached their eternal shore.

We are privy to their private guilt, masked pain, secret hopes and loves—things they normally do not share, but perhaps with one human being. Yet, by the prompting of the Holy Spirit, they have openly revealed to us what most men never do, their souls. We have the privilege of experiencing the exciting, exotic, and even intoxicating strength and vulnerability that exist within their hearts.

While *Of Men and Mary* may be about six males, it is for everyone, because it is also a book about a woman. That woman is the Blessed Virgin Mary. She is the boat of safety for all of us, the surest and safest passage to the heart of her Son. She is our victory and sweet reassurance that God's plan is infinitely better than our own; and she is our challenge to follow her Son, no matter the cost, no matter how fierce the battle. Read the stories of these brave men, and you will inevitably come away with a desire to climb in the boat with them and sail safely home.

HOW THIS BOOK CAME ABOUT

Before I became acquainted with any of the six men in *Of Men and Mary*, they had the courage to share their stories publicly—in intimate and amazing detail. Because of their unusual openness and vulnerability, even the darkest parts of their lives had become light for a confused and darkening world:

> *Take no part in the fruitless works of darkness; rather expose them, for it is shameful even to mention the things done by them in secret; but everything exposed by the light becomes visible, for everything that becomes visible is light.* (Eph 5:11-14a)

When I first heard these men's life stories, in person or through a screen, I thought with jaw ajar, "This is far too good for the world not to know." Propelled to move past my fear of annoying them, I asked if they might allow me to craft their stories in writing. They graciously agreed and the result has far surpassed even my most hopeful expectations. Chris Watkins—who by chance or providence has my name—artfully penned his own story, and I wrote the others from interviews and recordings.

My heartfelt thanks goes out to these extraordinary disciples: to Deacon Dave, Chris, and Fr. Rick, whom I befriended in the process, to Fr. Michael, and lastly to Jim Jennings and Fr. Paul, who have since passed into the next life. May God grant them eternal rest.

Also deserving of my thanks and praise are the kind, generous, and faithful editors at Queen of Peace Media: Anne Manyak, Dan Osanna, and Laura Dayton, who have made this book beautiful.

ONE

FATHER MICHAEL LIGHTNER

Tackled by the Blessed Mother

WHEN I WAS EIGHT, I had a vivid dream. I was playing for the Philadelphia Eagles against the Phoenix Cardinals. I saw the faces around me, the colors, the moves, every play. By the time I woke up, my life's aspirations had already been set on playing in the National Football League one day.

I am the youngest of eleven children (God always saves the best for last). My mom had four miscarriages, and one of my brothers died at birth, so I have five siblings in heaven, interceding for me, and five in this world, for whom I intercede (if you knew my family, you'd understand what I'm talking about). My dad was a convert, and my mom a daily communicant for most of her life. Priests would come to our home for Thanksgiving, Christmas, or simply to play Schmear, a popular card game in my home town of Oconto, Wisconsin. Catholicism was an expectation of my parents—"If you live in this home, you will go to church," which I fought against. When I'd hear, "We're going to go to church," "We're going to pray the Rosary," or any other Catholic "to do," my brow would lower, and my chest would clench. During our nightly family Rosary, I passive-aggressively dozed off, even as a young boy. The prayers were bringing me peace, but I could only think about how boring it all was, and how I wanted to sleep.

My faith was influenced more by a sports rival than by family. When my mom would come home from a kooky place called Medjugorje, with packs of twenty-five brown scapulars, I refused to wear one because, like all things related to faith in the family, it was forced on me. But when I was in high school and saw my football opponent, Jim Flanigan, wearing a brown scapular underneath his uniform, I was intrigued. Jim was an awesome dude who would go on to play for the Bears and the Packers. I'd never seen someone wear a scapular who wasn't—like, well—holy. I put one on and wouldn't take it off. If it broke, I had plenty more. By the time I finished college, I'd given hundreds of scapulars away to people who thought they were cool, and I told them of its promise from Our Lady: "Whosoever dies wearing this scapular shall not suffer eternal fire." I believed in the promise, so I believed in Mary. I just never felt her love.

When I was a fourteen-year-old in the eighth grade, I was six feet, four inches tall and 286 pounds, and football scouts started looking my way. When a high school head coach came and talked to my parents about inviting their son to play varsity, I jumped at the chance. In a short time, I was successful in all the high-school athletics I undertook, and by the end of my freshman year, I had already lettered in three varsity sports. In my senior year, I started getting attention from collegiate football recruiters around the country and decided to go to Eastern Michigan University, an NCAA Division 1 school in Ypsilanti. I couldn't turn down their offer of a full scholarship and graduated with a degree in sculpture—one of my passions.

Within my first couple of days at college, I said to myself, "Wow, my faith is my own! I get to do what I want." Church wasn't on my list, so at eighteen, I pushed my Catholic upbringing aside, and during that first school year, I received two painful blows to the heart. First, I got red-shirted: the coach kept me on the shelf for a year, which meant that I wasn't allowed to play in any football games, but I could practice with the team. And then I met a girl and fell in love. I gave her my heart, and when we broke up, my heart broke in two, as well.

So, what did I do on weekends? Party. Without the discipline and structure of travelling with the college team, and ripe to drown my sorrows, I went out with friends and started womanizing, drinking copious amounts of beer, and generally getting myself into trouble. I also turned to marijuana, and within a short time, alcohol and drugs became such an intrinsic part of my life that they took control of it.

For three years, I careened downhill. While any homegrown values I'd learned were slipping away, I started working in security for rock bands in different venues throughout Detroit. At 315 pounds, I was an asset to several security companies, so I decided to throw my "weight" around. Leveraging the security companies, I boasted, "I know where to get you seven three-hundred-pounders. Just give me more money." At concerts for heavy metal bands, such as Metallica, Rage Against the Machine, Suicidal Tendencies, and Nine Inch Nails, I was usually front stage, grabbing people and pulling them away from proximity to the musicians. I was protecting the guys who were raising their voices to a screaming pitch against God. Later in life, I would find out how long the nails were that pierced Christ's hands and feet: nine inches.

In my sophomore year, my coach had me playing in games and was throwing me kudos. During video replays, he was making comments, such as, "Watch Lightner on this block. This is how you run it." Because of my growing size and skills, it wasn't long before I was playing Division 1 American college football in big stadiums, supported by big money. I was well on my way to the National Football League.

While I was running up and down football fields, my mother had been running all the way to Yugoslavia (now Bosnia-Herzegovina) and back to see the Virgin Mary in a little town called Medjugorje. For this uncouth and screwball behavior, everyone in the family had given her a decisive diagnosis of "cuckoo." In the middle of my senior year, I went home for Thanksgiving, where my immediate and extended family were gathered, and before going to bed one night, I shoved a small hip sack of mine (I refuse to call it a "fanny pack") underneath the couch. My three-year-old niece found my sack the next morning and opened it up to look for a pencil. Pulling out a cellophane bag of something, she asked my mother, "Grandma, what's this?"

Asleep in a bedroom, I opened my eyes to see a cellophane bag of marijuana dangling above my head, and through the clear plastic, my mother's tear-streaked face. I froze. My sister, who was sitting at the edge of the bed—a substance-abuse counselor for the VA, at the time—razzed, "Ah, ha, ha, now you've gotta go to Medjugorje."

"That's a good idea," announced my mom. "You're going to Medjugorje with me this Christmas."

"God, no," I protested. Over the next couple of days, I thought of and threw out every excuse not to go that my creativity could muster. But my mom is a persistent woman. She asked me to go—she told me to go—she forced me to go. Although I believed she was absolutely insane, in order to get her off my back and stop her from crying, I finally surrendered.

That Christmas, we jumped on a plane in Detroit and flew to Zurich, Switzerland, where I arrived groggy and tired. "Oh, yeah," I sighed, "Finally, we're here."

My mom said, "No, we've got a four-hour layover, and then we get on our next flight."

Deflated, I imagined my plight of being squished, again, into a small seat, surrounded by none-too-happy people forced to sit next to the big, grumpy guy. When our next flight landed in Zagreb, Croatia, I exhaled, "Finally, we're here."

Mom said, "We've got an hour layover, and then we're on our next flight."

"Another flight?"

"We're flying to Split."

Once we landed, I exclaimed, "Finally, we're here!"

She said, "Get on the bus."

Pilgrims piled on the bus and started saying the Rosary. I went into sleep mode, like I always had. When I woke up, I looked out the window and saw a drop about four hundred feet down off a sheer cliff and heard myself saying, "Holy Mary, Mother of God, pray for us sinners, now and at the hour of our death. Amen."

We finally arrived in Medjugorje, and I was plumb exhausted. It had been a twenty-seven-hour trip. We settled into a home near Mount Krizevac (Cross Mountain), which pilgrims were climbing in droves in order to pray and do penance. Before we settled into a long and deep sleep, my mother looked at me and said with earnestness, "I only ask for one thing when you're here, that you to go to Confession—if not for you, then for me." I told her I would.

In the morning, all the "blue-hairs" looked overjoyed to be there, and I wondered, "What am I doing here? I'm not fitting in."

"Get in the car," Mom announced, "we're going to church."

I shot back, "I'll walk." I could see St. James Church about a mile and a quarter from the house where we were staying, and I wanted to make the trek alone. As I walked through a vineyard, I said my first real prayer: "God, if you exist, I do not know you. I have never seen you or heard you. I've never felt you or had an experience of you. You could be the biggest con that twelve drunk men ever started over 2,000 years ago. You've got seven days to prove yourself to me, otherwise I'm living my life the way I want to."

When I came to St. James, I found a sign on the door of a confessional inside the church that read, "English, Spanish, Italian." "I guess this is where I'm supposed to go," I thought, parking myself at the end of the

ONE: FATHER MICHAEL LIGHTNER

line. When my turn came, I entered a cramped space (albeit, many spaces are tight for me) and I knelt down. My mind pictured an eighty-year-old priest behind the screen in front me, and I intended to shock the old man, causing blood to run from his ears.

I told him that I didn't remember the formula for Confession, so he walked me through it. Then for thirty-five minutes, I gave him everything. I poured out every grizzly detail of my wayward adventures: drugs, alcohol, beating people up for a living, womanizing, stealing, lying—all ten of the broken commandments. When I finished confessing my sins, the priest sounded "unshocked," and I was shocked. He gave me some very simple advice and a penance of five "Our Fathers."

I was taken aback. Five "Our Fathers" wasn't enough. I did not feel worthy of God's love and imagined I'd be climbing Mount Krizevac thirty-three times.

The priest continued, "During each 'Our Father,' meditate on one of the five major wounds of Jesus: His hands, feet, and side. Can you do this?"

I said, "Of course," and he helped me to say an act of contrition, which I did not know.

As with any Confession, the priest then began to say the words of absolution: "God, the Father of mercies, through the death and Resurrection of His Son, reconciled the world to Himself and sent the Holy Spirit . . ." Upon hearing those words, I became aware of a physical Presence with me in the confessional. Then, all of a sudden, my body from the knees up was pushed far backward to a 30-degree angle, knocking my head on the back wall of the confessional, while my calves and feet were pinned underneath me. I was a six-foot-five, 325-pound man, who squatted over 600 pounds and benched well over 400, and I couldn't sit up or move my body in any direction, not even one inch.

The priest continued, ". . . And I absolve you from your sins, in the name of the Father, and of the Son, and of the Holy Spirit." With those words, I felt an intense pain in my heart, as if a spear were plunging into my chest, and a fierce internal struggle ensued. Screaming aloud in agony, I felt the "spear" get yanked out, and with it, my sins. Seconds later, my soul and body experienced a great release, and I was no longer immobilized.

"Oh, my God," I said to myself. "He's real."

Flabbergasted, I left the confessional and exited the church. It took me forty-five minutes to say five "Our Fathers," as I wept on my knees before a large cross, watching a puddle of tears form on the ground. Pictures of people I had hurt—especially women I'd used, flashed through my mind. I saw what my sin had done in their lives, and for the very first time, I felt deeply sorry. Those five "Our Fathers" were the hardest penance I have ever done.

Holy Mass had begun in the church, but I didn't know it. I was re-experiencing my confession, like a flashback to a tragedy, and when my senses finally entered into reality, I noticed that a priest was in the middle of his homily. His name was Fr. Stan Fortuna, and he had brought his guitar up to the pulpit, which I thought was pretty cool, so I said to Jesus, "Lord, help me hear what this priest has to say."

At that very moment, God gave me a mystical experience. I received an anointing so sublime that it was better than any drug, better than any sex, better than winning the big game. All of those feelings combined could be multiplied by a million and not touch what God was doing in my heart. I felt as though I were levitating and was afraid to open my eyes because I literally believed I was on the ceiling. It was my Pentecost. God's Spirit, with its divine gifts and blessings, entered my heart.

After twenty minutes of suspension in utter ecstasy, I slowly felt my normal senses return. When Mass ended, I stood up and walked outside in a daze. A woman, who had apparently witnessed what had happened to me, approached me and asked if I might pray over her. Never having done such a thing before, I reluctantly laid my hands on her head, and she immediately went limp, overwhelmed by the Holy Spirit. Shaken, I didn't understand what had happened and quickly fled the scene, like a criminal trying not to get caught.

❧　☙

Six months later, when I was close to finishing college, my mother asked if I wanted to travel again to Medjugorje for the fourteenth anniversary of the apparitions. Without hesitation, I said yes. On the third day of this pilgrimage, I took a day trip outside Medjugorje and traveled along a winding road to the Franciscan monastery of Široki Brijeg, about an hour's ride away. This time, I was more than willing to pray the Rosary on the bus. I was curious to see a priest with the gift of healing, named Fr. Jozo Zovko, who offered a program for pilgrims, at that time, consisting of Mass, talks, and healing prayers. Fr. Jozo had been the pastor of St. James when the alleged Medjugorje apparitions began. At first, he didn't believe the young visionaries and questioned them relentlessly. Then God spoke to him one day in the church while he was agonizing over what to believe regarding the "apparition fanaticism" of his parishioners. God said clearly, "Come out and protect the children." Obeying the voice without hesitation, he opened a side door to St. James, and in that very moment, the visionaries ran toward him, escaping persecution from the pursuing police. The moment was a decisive turning point and a personal revelation for Fr. Jozo, who now believed that the children were, indeed, seeing the Mother of God.

At Široki Brijeg, I took a small detour with a friend of mine, Rick Wendell, who later became a priest. Together, we walked around the right side of the monastery and came upon an unmarked stone cave. Descending several stone steps toward it, I grew overwhelmed by a stark feeling of sadness and pain. Compelled to pray, I knelt down with Rick in the blackness of the cave's hollow, where we said the Sorrowful Mysteries of the Rosary. There, each of us, unbeknownst to the other, experienced the exact same staggering vision. Suddenly my heart began beating wildly with terror. I was no longer myself, but a Franciscan seminarian dressed in a brown habit. Soldiers aimed their rifles at me, and I trembled in fear for my life. At that moment, in real time, I fully believed that I was going to die alongside Rick in that cave. In the vision, I was shot by automatic weapon fire, dragged out by my ankles, and piled on top of my Franciscan brothers in the cave. Then gasoline was poured over the top of me, and I was lit on fire to the mocking sound of the soldiers' laughter.

Only later did Rick and I learn the following story. On February 7, 1945, during World War II, Communist soldiers arrived at the Široki Brijeg monastery and announced to the thirty Franciscan seminarians and priests who lived there, "God is dead. There is no God, there is no Pope, there is no Church, there is no need of you. Go out into the world and work" (notwithstanding that most of the Franciscans were teaching at the adjoining school, and some of them were well-known professors and authors). The soldiers then ordered the Franciscans to remove their brown habits. But they refused. One angry cadet took a crucifix off the wall, threw it at their feet and said, "This is your last chance. Now you can choose either life or death." One by one, each of the Franciscans knelt down, embraced Jesus on the crucifix and said, "You are my God and my all." Then all thirty of them, six of whom were only twenty years old, went forth to their death in song, some of them singing Salve Regina, others the Litany of Our Lady—all of them blessing their executioners and forgiving them. Then the soldiers shot them point blank and set them on fire in the cave.

At the time of our concurrent vision, Rick and I knew none of this. Shaken and confused by what had overcome us, we rushed to get a priest who blessed us and threw holy water and holy salt into the darkness of the cave. Instinctively, I clutched my brown scapular, and I thanked Mary for her protection and her love, which I was no longer taking for granted. That harrowing vision has never left me and gave me a lasting impression that to some, human life is not the slightest bit important.

Rick and I walked back into the church sanctuary of the monastery. There, we witnessed Fr. Jozo laying his hands on the priests who were present, in preparation for them to lay their hands on the many pilgrims who had formed a circle around the inside of the large stone church. As the priests dispersed to pray over the people, I instinctively followed a little Capuchin who reminded me of St. Padre Pio. When that priest began laying his hands on the pilgrims' heads to impart his blessing, they started falling down one after another. Figuring I should use my size and strength to be of help, I began to catch the people collapsing like ragdolls underneath his touch. Within fifteen minutes, he must have knocked down over 200 pilgrims, and I was getting tired. "Lord," I begged. "Slow it down. Let me catch up."

In that moment, the priest slowed down. He came to a woman in a wheelchair, and kneeling before her in faith, began to bless her head, shoulders, hips, thighs, knees, calves, and ankles, probably her toes, too. Relieved, I sat down near the two of them to rest and was approached by the woman's husband, who shared with me, "My wife was in a car accident seven years ago, and her spinal cord separated into two pieces. Then six months later, spinal meningitis hit her and deteriorated her spinal cord below. For seven years, she hasn't moved a muscle beneath her waist." I looked down at the woman's legs. They had atrophied to the size of my wrist.

Doubts crowded my mind: "She is not going to get up. Why is Father wasting his time? It is medically impossible for this woman to walk."

24

Sitting in an uncomfortable, cold sweat from the exertion of catching falling human beings, I started to look for other things to do. Where was Fr. Jozo? Maybe he needed help. . . But then my attention would be drawn back to the woman. I felt as though God had a string attached to my heart, and every once in a while, he would tug it. This tug-of-war lasted several minutes, as I sought out a distraction, something else to do, and he focused my sights back on this woman and the priest, who was continuously blessing her. I felt completely at his mercy.

Fed up and full of arrogance, I prayed flippantly, "What, Lord! What do you want? Do you want me to pray for this woman?"

Silence.

"Well, then, I will. Get her up out of her wheelchair. Show us your power."

Then I heard God speak: "Michael, if I get this woman up and make her walk, will you enter the seminary?"

"Absolutely not."

Twenty tumultuous minutes passed as I squirmed in my seat, agonizing over the thought of priesthood because football was my God. "I've got an NFL career ahead of me. I'm two years away from entering the draft. Do you think I'm crazy? Give all that up? Give up the goal of my life?"

Silence.

Finally, my heart warmed a little, and I thought to myself, "Well, it would be pretty cool to see her get up and walk." But I decided to change the rules, so I said, "Okay, Father. If you get her up out of her wheelchair and walk her around this entire church, I will enter the seminary."

In five seconds, she was up on her feet without anyone telling her to do so. Then she grabbed the back of her wheelchair and started taking a lap around the church. "What are you doing!?" my mind panicked. "Why are you doing this?! Somebody stop her! Somebody tackle her!" Wandering in desperation to the center aisle of the church, I decided to quickly change the deal. The floor in the Široki Brijeg church was made up of blocks of grey slate, so I focused on a small block near the Tabernacle and got more specific: "If she doesn't step on that tile, I'm not going!" The woman came to the front of the church, planted both feet on that very tile, and plopped back down in her wheelchair.

A few expletives escaped my lips, and I walked out of the church to sob. "You know my dream, Lord," I cried. "Why would you take it away from me?"

For three years, I suffered. An internal battle raged in my soul, while God continued to encourage me with hundreds and hundreds of affirmations of my call to the priesthood. God threw out the red carpet of confirmations when the Servant of God, Maria Esperanza, who received apparitions of the Virgin Mary (along with the gifts supernatural knowledge, healing, visions, discernment of spirits, locution, ecstasy, levitation, the odor of sanctity, the stigmata, and the ability to read the hearts of others—just to name a few) stopped in mid-translation when I attended one of her talks. Feeling impatient, I got up to leave when she grabbed me and said, "You have the face of a priest."

Before my college years ended, I was recruited by the Cleveland Browns football team. I would have been well on my way to a career in pro football were God not getting in the way. For this stubborn young man, hundreds of confirmations weren't enough, so I took many more trips to Medjugorje where I saw many more marvels—the blind seeing, the deaf hearing. I've been a witness to all the miracles of the Gospel, with the exception of one: walking on water. But we do that in Wisconsin in the wintertime.

One of the greatest miracles happened in a one-of-a-kind confirmation during the last game of college football that I played. While I was walking to the line of scrimmage, looking at the faces across from me, I thought, "Oh my goodness, I know these men." But I had never seen them before, never played against that team. I crouched down in a three-point stance on the offensive line to block for the runners and the quarterback, as this strange sense of déjà vu took over. I was remembering something that never happened.

For the next twenty minutes, I could literally see the next ten plays in my mind before they occurred. I knew what play would be called in the huddle; I knew what play would happen next; I knew how many yards we were going to get; and I knew if we were going to score on the drive. We won the game 22-18. I knew that, too. Frightened, I thought I was going absolutely bonkers. Back in the locker room, while my teammates celebrated, I put a towel over my head and cried, fearing that too many drugs and knocks to the head had blown out my mind.

That night, a party was held at my home—the "football house," to which only 400 people showed up (and yes, there was beer), but my spirit couldn't enjoy the festivities. At about midnight, I'd had enough, so I went to my room, locked the door, prayed my Rosary, and fell asleep. At 3 a.m., I had a dream. It was of the same ten plays from the game that day, the same twenty minutes during which I could see glimpses of the future. While I slept, God showed me that this was the same dream I'd had when I was eight years old. We were in a huge stadium; our team uniforms were just like the Philadelphia Eagles; their team uniforms were just like the Arizona Cardinals. I had assumed, therefore, as a child, that I was seeing and experiencing myself playing in a pro football game. I woke up in amazement. Then God spoke to me again: "This was your dream. It has been fulfilled. Now mine—priesthood."

In 2005, I was ordained a Catholic priest by Archbishop Timothy Dolan, now Cardinal Dolan, and I've never been happier. I thank God to this day that I did not play football because in this world, there are so many distractions from God. American football was a distraction for me. Priesthood, on the other hand, is life for me, and life to the fullest.

TWO

FATHER RICK WENDELL

The Man Who Died before He Lived

IT'S A MIRACLE I'M ALIVE. I grew up a thrill-seeker. When life got too mundane, I'd test its limits. My friends and I had our own versions of extreme sports. We started out with rope swings over the river, and then over cliffs. We fought each other with BB guns and played toss with fireworks, which blew off my friend's hand. We went camping in weather twenty-degrees below and drove at speeds over a hundred. Four of my high school friends died in high-speed car wrecks, but that didn't slow me down.

The result: three operations on each of my wrists, five surgeries on my left knee, one on my right, two broken ankles, a separated left shoulder from jumping off of freight trains, and a snapped collarbone from performing flying bicycle stunts—not with a decked-out mountain bike, but a Schwinn with a banana seat. My mother said she was just trying to keep me alive. When I was sixteen, wearing my Boy Scout uniform with a merit-badge sash and driving my '69 Ford Mustang, a police officer chased me down, jumped out of his car, pointed his gun at me, and yelled, "Put your hands on the roof, kid!" I "didn't know" how to drive a car unless it was going full blast. My parents absolutely forbade me to have a motorcycle, so when I turned eighteen, I made sure to get one. It only took me a few months to spin out in a death-dealing crash followed by eight hours of surgery. After that, people began saying, "God is saving you for something special." "Nah," I thought. "I'm just lucky."

Achievements came easy. Mom found me poring over her medical books when I was five. I sculpted, appreciated fine art, played leads in musicals, and was captain of our high-school hockey team, with the temper to go with it. I was truly a Renaissance kid in a good sense, but my personal morals flew all over the map. At the end of my senior year at Hill-Murray High School in Maplewood, Minnesota, I went to five proms with four girls. After having gone with one of my girlfriends to each other's proms, we unexpectedly saw each other again with different dates at a third prom. When I graduated, five hundred people paid to come to my party, replete with a live band, porta-potties, and four sixteen-gallon kegs of beer—to start.

Coming from a practicing Catholic family, it was assumed that my two brothers and I would say grace before meals, prayers before bedtime, and attend parochial schools. Being late for Mass was not an option because mother would make us sit in the front row. Not my idea of a thrill. Since businesses weren't open on Sundays in the 1960s due to the blue laws, our family would have a formal meal at grandma's house after Mass every Sunday. Catholicism was a family given, but my 1970s Catholic high school faith formation was dangerously thin and punctured with holes. "God loves you," we were told. "You'll figure it out."

I spent my first year of college homebound, doing independent study connected with the nearby University of Wisconsin because I had forty-five pounds of plaster on three broken limbs. When I recovered, I couldn't get away from home fast enough, so I escaped to St. John's University, a Catholic college in Collegeville, Minnesota. I didn't witness any examples of faith among the monks on campus, and we students weren't required to go to Mass on Sundays, so we didn't. My immorality mushroomed because of the lack of moral guidance, and I became increasingly disillusioned with the idea of faith. Intellectually, I couldn't prove that God didn't exist; but He wasn't relevant in my life, and he or she, or whatever, certainly wasn't important enough for me to modify my behavior.

Although I'd been told God was all love, I never felt him and certainly didn't understand him as a loving father, perhaps because I never experienced my own father's love. The only time Dad told me he loved me was on Christmas Day after downing a couple bottles of champagne. Even though I was always an honor student, was voted outstanding artist in high school for my sculpting and pottery, and excelled in sports, especially contact sports, Dad never came out to watch a single one of my games and couldn't find his way to offer a hug or a compliment. Rather, he criticized me. When I was fourteen, my father hit me for the last time, perhaps because I was getting bigger and stronger, or perhaps because my smile of sheer rage immobilized him. I swore in my heart that day that I would kill him if he touched me again (a curse I placed on myself that had to later be broken by Jesus Christ).

After earning a Bachelor of Science pre-med degree from the University of Wisconsin in River Falls, I worked for a short time in a hospital emergency room to build my résumé in order to attend medical school (like my mom had). Late one Saturday night after I'd survived another terrible motorcycle crash, the contract doctor in the emergency room, whom I deemed very cool, sat me down and said, "Rick, you can do this job. You have the ability. But being a physician is not what I do, it's who I am. And I'm not sure that you would be happy." I listened and instead sought out the deepest snow available, which I found in Little Cottonwood Canyon, Utah. Between hitting the slopes in wintertime as a professional skier, and lifeguarding and riding Harley Davidsons in the summer, my days became a living cliché of sex, drugs, and rock 'n' roll.

In my opinion, there was only one way to go—full on, top speed— ready to risk my very life for the next thrill. It was the 80s, when cocaine use was fashionable, not criminal, in certain crowds. I showed up in places within the drug trade where no one should go, and I met with people no one should see, for the spirit of evil within them was palpable. I attempted feats so perilous that if I didn't complete them, I would die. Perched on one ski, atop a three-hundred-foot cliff, I stopped twenty-five feet away from plunging to my death. My face was a historical map of cuts and scrapes, and every inch of my back had been bruised or lacerated—the markings of a young man trying to prove himself to a father who didn't care. But the biggest scars were on my heart.

When I found out that I could make better money in construction than lifeguarding, I left the slopes of Utah to form a little construction company back home in Minnesota. By age twenty-seven, I had fifteen men working for me, building high-end, custom, golf-course homes. Enjoying the income, I purchased my family home, a waterfront property, and decorated it with a big boat and a string of cars and motorcycles. I was young, in shape, arrogant, and everything I tried to do I could do well. The world shouted success at me with my possessions, money, power, and popularity, not to mention girlfriends. In time, I was engaged to be married to my trophy girl—the prettiest and wealthiest one of them all. To add to her good qualities, she could pound booze almost as hard as I could and liked the same stuff on pizza.

By the late 1980s, my mother was living with me because my dad, after thirty years of marriage, had served her with divorce papers. The stress gave her a heart attack and sent her to the hospital, where my father refused to visit. With me in the family home, she recuperated after her angioplasty, and I hosted her, not because I was a great son, but because the arrangement was convenient.

My home rested on a river bluff and needed over a thousand railroad ties to hold up the embankment. One sunny, Friday afternoon, as one of my workers and I were fastening a couple ties together with a fourteen-inch steel nail, my sledge hammer came down hard, but I missed hitting the nail, and it went flying, gouging me deeply in the face. Following the protocol natural to my Ski Patrol training, I had my mom drive me to the hospital, where I was stitched up without incident. When I was released, Mom picked me up, drove five blocks, and stopped at a grocery store. Being the demanding, controlling type, I sat in the car begrudgingly. Life was on my time clock, and I needed to go back to work, make out some checks for my employees, and get on with things.

While I was waiting, my heart began to race, and it wouldn't slow down. I thought perhaps I was suffering from heatstroke. The beating in my chest grew so persistent that I got out of the car, walked toward the store, and when I stepped through the automatic doors, my body started to collapse. Grabbing a clerk, I said, "You're going to have to do CPR," and then I lost consciousness. An ambulance happened to be a block and a half away at a fire station, so when the clerk dialed 911, paramedics arrived immediately. My mother came quickly to the scene and knew all of the ambulance workers because she used to run the hospital laboratory: "Just ship him!" she shouted. "Don't even assess him. Put him on the gurney and take him to emergency."

But before the ambulance could get out of the parking lot, I coded: my body went into cardiopulmonary arrest. The emergency team shocked me three times with paddles, trying to bring me back to consciousness. They intubated me, inserting a tracheal tube down my windpipe. They put in peripheral lines for an IV and gave me oxygen to try and get my blood pressure up. They performed manual, closed-chest compressions on my heart, which had completely stopped. But nothing worked. I was clinically dead.

The paramedics then charged the paddles and applied electrical shocks to my heart to return it to rhythm. It was at 3 p.m. on a Friday. They rushed me into the emergency room. None of the ambulance crew left my side. When the new shift workers came on, they joined the second-shift crew, and together they worked on me furiously, trying to bring me back to life.

I was only thirty years old and in great shape, and the heart attack I had was called a "witnessed arrest" because I coded in their presence. This type of cardiac event has a high probability of resuscitation, but they couldn't get me to have my own sinus rhythm—my regular heartbeat. I was not breathing on my own. I was gone, killed by an anaphylaxis reaction to the anesthesia used for my stitches.

A person's blood PH, which indicates how much oxygen the body is getting, is normally 7.4. When it drops below seven, life-saving procedures are often terminated because permanent and irreversible brain damage has occurred. My blood PH descended to 6.4, which is called acidosis and is inconsistent with life. However, I was an organ donor and had AB positive blood, a type that is found in less than 2 percent of the population. Consequently, I was very valuable in parts.

Because they didn't have an apparatus that compresses the heart, normally referred to as a "thumper," the team had to rotate giving me manual chest compressions. Ernie, the respiratory tech, squeezed the bag of oxygen with his bare hands for several hours. The staff in the lab, who had worked under my mother until her poor health prevented it, wouldn't show her the lab reports because every indication was I was brain dead. They were no longer trying to save my life. They were attempting to stabilize my body so that it could be shipped to a harvest center in St. Paul, Minnesota, where they would eventually pronounce me brain dead and harvest my organs.

My mother was assembling the family around me: my fiancée, my two brothers (one who flew in from out of state), and my dad. My father had waited a couple hours until he was done with work at 4:30 before leaving to visit because I'd been in the hospital so many times before and had always come through fine. But when he arrived, the staff said to him, "Put down your flowers and your card, and go say goodbye." He later told me that when he laid his hand on mine, I was cool to his touch and turning blue-gray in color.

Within the family, none of us had been going to church. My mother was angry with God because my father was divorcing her, and "bad things don't happen to good people." My father, brothers, and I were CEO Catholics (Christmas and Easter Only), and even then, we attended Mass for reasons of culture, not faith. My mother felt very alone at fifty-six, with no brothers or sisters or close relatives, and family meant everything to her. Into this climate, she begged God with her whole being and cried out,

"Lord, I need him. I'm alone in the world. He's my first-born son. But if you need him, take him. If you give him back to me, give him back to me whole, or don't give him to me at all." Hanging onto hope, she and my fiancée were yelling at me, "You are loved, and you cannot leave!"

I can remember passing out in the store entrance. Then my next recollection is of lying on my back with a man leaning over the top of me, pushing on my chest; but I couldn't feel it. This didn't disturb me. I simply took note of it. I was looking up at a swinging IV bag and wood-colored cabinets, which lined the interior of the ambulance, but my vision had expanded to include a perfect perception of what should have been in my peripheral vision. I could see everything without turning my head. There was an excited conversation happening, but somehow, I wasn't listening to it. I was not emotional at all. And then I went through the picture, so to speak. This is where human words fail in describing what was happening to me. I went from observing the scene to passing through to the other side of it—into blackness, nothingness. I wasn't scared, I wasn't happy, I wasn't sad. I was just observing, yet I was within what I was seeing. Then, in what seemed like the distance, but wasn't, there was light. I don't know whether I went toward it, or it came toward me, because distance, space, and time cannot describe what I was experiencing. The light was just there. It had no visible source, and its brightness was beyond blinding and yet soft on my eyes. It cannot be described by color or wavelength or anything that we use to describe light here on earth because it was infinitely more.

Soon I was amidst this light. Intuitively, I understood that I was in the presence of God. I didn't simply think this, I knew this, beyond and before any question I'd ever had. I knew that God is. God is the most obvious thing there could possibly be. I also knew instantaneously that one human lifespan is but a blink within that reality, and yet this life that each person is given by God is profoundly important. What we do with it is critical, as if life were a test, but not one that we pass or fail, a test of who we are.

Somehow, I simply knew things without having to think about them. Only years later did I learn that this kind of knowing is called "infused knowledge," a term coined by St. Thomas Aquinas wherein knowledge comes from one direction only—God. The mind doesn't deliberate over a subject and arrive at a conclusion, but simply knows and comprehends, without any effort or receptivity of its own.

At the most fundamental level, I also apprehended God's answer to Moses' question to the burning bush, "What should I call you?"—"I am

Who Am." In a like way, I understood Revelation 1:8: "I am the Alpha and the Omega, the one who is and who was and who is to come, the almighty." I knew that there was no beginning or ending to him. God doesn't change, and everything that is—is because God is. Nothing is separate from God, nothing at all. God is present in all things and at all times because God exists outside of time. Time for us is only a construct that we use to help us understand our relationship with the things we experience and observe, how we interact with and respond to the physical aspects of creation. There is a certain reality to the changing of the seasons, the rising and setting of the sun, the influence of the moon and the reality of the tides. We relate to time by making watches and calendars, by following lunar cycles and navigating the stars. But all this is relative. As a thing unto itself, time does not exist.

The most profound part of my experience, by far, was knowing that God is Love. Never had I realized that I could be loved like that—with a love so perfect, so pure, so intense, so marvelous that nothing else mattered. My dad loved me, but he hadn't been able to express it because his own father had not taught him how to love, nor his father before him. Dad couldn't bring himself to do so much as tell me I was a good boy. My fiancée loved me, and I loved her, at least as much as we knew of romantic love. My mother was thinking of love when she had me baptized on Valentine's Day in 1960. I was the first child who leapt in her womb, a child she named after her beloved father. Mom adored me and was the image of love in our family.

Yet nothing was like this! I was in the presence of a love so intense that I didn't care about anything else. . . There was no need for anything else. This Love was absolutely fulfilling in every way, a love that I had always looked for but never found, a love one would never want to be separated from. I was created to love and to be loved because God is Love. This fundamental truth is written into every human heart. Everyone knows what it feels like not to have that place fulfilled, and we will try and fill it with anything that even masquerades as love but isn't. But there is a place in our hearts, a throne, really, that only this Love can fulfill. I never comprehended such a perfect love until I was immersed in it. In God's presence, I wanted only to be loved by him and to love him in return.

My encounter with God occurred while I lay clinically dead in the hospital for over two and a half hours, without a functioning brain, without my own heartbeat or my own breathing. I would not respond to coma stimuli: the infliction of pain to elicit a response. My eyes did not react to light; my pupils were fixed but not yet dilated.

Then without warning, my soul was ripped away from the magnificent light, and I felt as if I were falling downward. I reached up for the light because I didn't want to be parted from it. With my mother on one side and my fiancée on the other, telling me that I was loved and that I could not leave, my arm came up off the gurney and wrapped around them. In a flash, my heart started beating on its own and my breathing resumed. My eyes started reacting to the hospital lights, and my normal skin color returned. The doctors were shocked. In fact, the entire staff have since spoken to me, asking me to tell them what happened because none of them believed my return was possible. I had gone from being a corpse to a strong man attempting to sit up and get off the gurney. In fact, I was trying so fiercely to get back to the light that the staff had to tie me down so I wouldn't pull out all of the lines stuck in my body.

Still in various states of shock and disbelief after seeing a dead man come alive, the staff knew they had to redouble their efforts. They quickly ushered me into the same ambulance with the crew that had never left, and drove me twenty-two miles to a larger hospital with more cardiac support, where they placed me in the ICU to be closely monitored. The fact that I had become conscious again was no guarantee that there was not permanent brain damage. By the time my family caught up with me, I was sitting up in bed, perfectly healthy. When my mother walked in, she scanned my body, peered at my face, and asked, "Are you still in there?"

"Yes, mom," I responded. "But I died." I died on a Friday afternoon at 3 p.m. At the time, I knew nothing of how Jesus had appeared to Sr. Faustina Kowalska, the saint of Divine Mercy, and told her that 3 o'clock in the afternoon on Friday was the hour of mercy: the hour that Jesus died and gave his life for us on the Cross so that we might live. I was thirty years old and a carpenter by trade.

The following day, doctors ran me through a battery of tests—CAT scans, stress tests, etc., which left them baffled. Not a trace of residual damage could be found. In the meantime, a parade of visitors stopped by. One was my fiancée's half-brother, a Missouri Synod Lutheran missionary, who along with his wife and children, created a computer-generated banner for me. After asking the Lord for an appropriate Bible verse, they were inspired to write on the banner, "Psalm 25:4-6," underneath the words, "Get well soon!" I thanked them kindly. Being a "good Catholic,"

I had no idea where psalms were in the Bible! Were they in the New Testament? The Old Testament? Someone left the room and returned with *The Good News Bible*. Careful to make distracting small talk, I quickly thumbed through it, beginning with the Old Testament, and came upon the Psalms. Pulling out a greeting card, I marked Psalm 24, intending to read it later, and placed the Bible on the nightstand.

Then the really weird events started to happen. At dawn on the Lord's Day, my third day in the hospital, I had a mystical experience, a dream that was not a dream. In it, I relived the experience of dying. My body began to writhe in intense mental and spiritual anguish as I felt the loss of my life. Horrified, I received the spiritual and true knowledge that if I had gone to judgment, my life was forfeit. Instead of experiencing union with God in the way that I had, I would have received an eternal sentence: banishment! For years, I had scared myself "to death" by doing extreme sports, but nothing I'd ever experienced remotely came close to my reaction. A paralyzing terror ripped through my being, causing my heart rate to skyrocket and my blood pressure to shoot up. It was a fear like I'd never known. For a fleeting moment, I experienced the complete abandonment and separation from God and others, without the hope of ever being reunited. I was going to be cast out, without parole, into a lonely, solitary torment forever because through my thoughts, words, and actions, I chose hell without consciously knowing that I had. I would not wish this experience on my worst enemy.

None of us think that we're that bad. We assume that there is always someone worse than we are, that perhaps that other person might deserve hell. Or we think that no one deserves hell. Many of us are taught to believe that God so loves the world, or at least me, that he would never send anyone, or at least not me, to hell. Or perhaps we believe that hell does not exist. We are wrong. At our own personal judgment, which none of us can escape, we will know full-well where we are lacking and what destiny suits our soul.

As I lay shaking in my hospital bed, I reached with a trembling hand for the Bible, opened it up to my marked page of Psalm 25, and read:

> Show me your ways, LORD,
>   teach me your paths.
> Guide me in your truth and teach me,
>   for you are God my Savior,

and my hope is in you all day long.
Remember, LORD, your great mercy and love,
    for they are from of old.
Do not remember the sins of my youth
    and my rebellious ways;
according to your love remember me,
    for you, LORD, are good.

There was a tangible presence in the room. It began to guide my hand to different passages of the Scriptures, all in the Old Testament. None were of my own choosing or by accident. I read of Israel being driven into exile and then returning, of being banished from its inheritance and then restored, and I somehow knew that Israel was me. Tears began streaming down my face.

Then I heard an interior voice that penetrated my whole being. I knew exactly who it was. With ultimate authority and tremendous force, it commanded, "STAND UP!" I immediately stood up with my Bible. One does not disobey He who is Command. Then he led me to read passages about his grace and mercy, ending with: ". . . Jesus said, 'This sickness will not end in death. No, it is for God's glory so that God's Son may be glorified through it'" (John 11:14).

Then I heard his voice again: "For this, you must give glory and praise to God," and every passage, every word, every phrase changed to the theme of giving praise. In time, I read:

"When he came near Jerusalem, at the place where the road went down the Mount of Olives, the large crowd of his disciples began to thank God and praise him in loud voices for all the great things that they had seen: 'God bless the king who comes in the name of the Lord! Peace in heaven and glory to God!'

Then some of the Pharisees in the crowd spoke to Jesus. 'Teacher,' they said, 'command your disciples to be quiet!'

Jesus answered, 'I tell you that if they keep quiet, the stones themselves will start shouting'" (Luke 19:37-40).

Then, suddenly, words of praise started coming out of my mouth, out loud and unpremeditated. I was freaked out. I mean, who does that? By this time, I was sobbing. The situation was highly, hugely emotional for me. There was a big presence in the room, and it wasn't me. I had a cardiac sending unit in my hospital garment chest pocket, relaying my heartbeat, and I couldn't help but think, "What are the nurses picking up from their monitors? Because this stuff just doesn't happen to people, certainly not to a Midwestern custom-home builder with an impressive list of sins and a potty mouth."

With the praise of God emitting from my mouth, tears streaming down my cheeks, and snot pouring out of my nose, I was in bad need of some toilet tissue, and there was just no way to "sleeve it." If you don't cry often—which I didn't—you don't cry well. I walked into the bathroom, and the theme changed again. This time, the interior voice said, "This is what you have done with your life. . . Now give me your life. ON YOUR KNEES."

I knelt down in front of the bathroom mirror and stared at myself, attempting to do a reality check. It was still dawn. I was still me. I looked around at the steel grey, four-inch tile, the cream-colored grout, the Formica patterns, the tilted mirror mounted in stainless steel, the call box with a cord that hung to the floor with a white plastic tip, and I asked myself, "Am I having some kind of an emotional breakdown? If you go through intense physical trauma, does it release some crazy brain chemicals? Am I just being emotional? Am I just afraid to die?"

The voice responded to my thoughts and kindly, but directly and unmistakably, said, "No. You know exactly who is talking to you, and you know that this is real. Don't you feel a little foolish asking this question?"

I simply let out a peaceful sigh and thought, "Okay. At this moment, my life merits hell and not heaven. This is what I've done with my life." All grew quiet. I didn't know what to do. Like most people after experiencing an earth-shattering event, I wanted to talk to somebody. But who? I didn't know anyone who knew God. I didn't hang out with those people. I was guilty of the life of the comfortable. I didn't care about God or anybody else, only myself.

Dying soldiers on battlefields, more than for any other human being, cry out for their mothers. So, I called my mom. I don't recollect the conversation we had, but Mom did. Later, she would tell me that she gave me words of support and consolation, and then my voice changed. "That was for me," I told her, "and now this is for you. . ." Then I read something out of Scripture that I cannot remember, but it so struck her heart that she knew she had to pray for my father for the rest of her life—which she immediately began to do. She and my father had parted with such venom that neither would talk to the other. Can you imagine the impact on our local church and our family, when years later, they showed up at church together? By that time, my father had developed episodic dementia. On Easter Sunday of 1995, he was restored to the home, and right up to his death, my parents united as one in marriage in a better way than they ever had before.

I left the hospital on Sunday, June 24, 1990, in the same skin, with the same address and the same business, but everything was different. I knew that God truly existed, and I was in him; he was in me. None of creation was a mistake—a random cosmic accident, where a bunch of cosmogonic dust happened to blow together nicely, and on we crawled out of a swamp. Rather, all of Creation was an intentional act of Almighty God. What I did within it was infinitely important. So, what was I going to do with my life now? Nothing but God mattered. What did a boat matter? A fancy house? Achievements? They didn't bring me anything. What's more, I didn't want to be on earth. I longed to go home to heaven, but I didn't know how to get there.

The following day, Monday, I flipped open the Bible, and the pages landed on Chapter 11 of John, the raising of Lazarus. My eyes fell on verse 25:

"Jesus said to her [Martha, a sister of Lazarus], 'I am the resurrection and the life. The one who believes in me will live, even though they die; and whoever lives by believing in me will never die. Do you believe this?'"

My response was, unhesitatingly, "Yes. I believe this." Then Jesus continued to lead me to more passages. This time, all in the Gospel of John.

"Do you know the Father?" he asked.

"Yep, met him Sunday."

"I and the Father are One" (John 10:30).

"I am the way and the truth and the life. No one comes to the Father except through me" (John 14:6).

Period. That's when the promise was given to me. My future was heaven. An interior recognition branded itself into my being that God is sovereign and that Jesus Christ is Lord. When that happens to a soul, it is salvation. I hadn't understood any of these things until God revealed them to me through Sacred Scripture.

Thus began my journey of faith in Christ. All I knew was that Jesus was Savior, the Bible was God's Word, God could talk to me through

Scripture, and God talked to sinners who weren't worthy of him one bit. I didn't know if the Catholic faith was the correct way to get to God, so I did my own investigating. I went to Mass with the "frozen chosen." I went to the Sacrament of Reconciliation where the priest, through no fault of his own, gave me a penance of five "Hail Mary's." I reeled. "Dude!" I wanted to say. "Five 'Hail Mary's' wouldn't even touch the first nasty thought I had in my head this morning!"

As I wandered through the world, it seemed to me that most everything human beings were doing to one another and to God was wrong and ridiculous. On my worst days, I even thought about walking in front of a bus to achieve my goal of eternal life, but then reminded myself that life comes from God and is sacred. It was not my choice to end it.

Not long after that, my fiancée's mother gave me a book about the alleged apparitions of the Virgin Mary in "Medjahoochee," or "Medgegookie." (None of us from North America knows how to say Medjugorje, pronounced me-ju-gó-rya.) The book was by Fr. Joseph Pelletier on the first five days of the apparitions in this small town in Bosnia-Herzegovina, the former Yugoslavia. When I read it, I wasn't at all skeptical, and thought, "If something this incredible is going on in the world today, I want to be like the apostle Thomas and go put my fingers in the Lord's wounds." I wanted to "touch" Mary's presence. I'd heard about Fatima and Lourdes and other sights of Marian apparitions, but they were far away and long ago. The Medjugorje apparitions had begun in 1981. "Are they still happening?" I wondered.

One day, I walked into the cathedral in St. Paul, Minnesota, where I was to be married in a few months. Not a soul was inside. My heart sank, and I wanted to shout out to the multitudes, "There really is a God! He is real! How many people have been baptized here, married here, ordained here? Is there no one to worship God with all their heart in return?" Looking down, I noticed a small piece of paper on the ground and picked it up. It was a pamphlet for a novena called the "never-fail novena"— sounded to me like the best one. The instructions said it was to be prayed for nine days in a church, so not knowing what else to do with myself, I began to pray it.

On the fifth day of the novena, I couldn't find an open church and ended up dialing a convent. The nun who answered was nice enough to give me the key to a rundown church next door, whose pastor was overseeing construction of a new one. When I walked in, I couldn't find the light switch, and the only light available came from the sanctuary lamp next to the Tabernacle. Something whispered into my mind, "Jesus is present," so I walked toward the flickering candle, making my way over ripped carpet and fallen ceiling tiles. Kneeling before the Tabernacle, I said wistfully. "Lord, I know you're here. I know that you are listening. But I don't know how to get to you. Lord, please, I don't want to be here on Earth."

All of a sudden, I wasn't alone. For the first time since I had been pulled away from the light of God, I felt a tender reassurance that all would be okay. My peace and comfort would not come from standing in front of large crowds, shouting out that I believed, and that they should too. It would come from spending time alone in front of the True Presence of Jesus, night after night, in prayer.

A few days later, as I was saying my novena prayers, kneeling by the soft flame of the Tabernacle candle, suddenly the lights came on. A group of people had heard about my phone call to the nun, asking to pray in the church, and had seen this as a confirmation from God to gather and pray the Rosary in support of the troops of Desert Storm One. They invited me to join them. I knew of the Rosary but had no relationship with it, except to receive the string of beads as gifts for my Baptism, First Holy Communion, Confirmation, and to notice it dangling from rearview mirrors.

As I prayed with the group, week after week, I began to see the Rosary differently. It was no longer a string of pretty beads, but a profound meditation on the mysteries of the faith and a means to pray to God constantly. When the Rosary ended, members would sometimes stand in a circle and pray aloud in the Spirit for the needs of the world and those present. One such time, a man and a woman looked my way and said, "You have a special calling to go to Medjugorje." I had asked them earlier about Medjugorje, and they didn't seem to know much about it, so I found it a bit unusual that they would make that kind of a statement. "Yeah, right," I thought. "How would they know I have a 'calling.' And what does that mean, anyway? Is this some kind of special lingo, like other businesses have?"

Sensing my disbelief, they added, "No, really. If you decide to go, Mary will pay for it."

"Fanatics," I concluded. A few days later, I called an old, party-hard friend from high school, named Vicki, who went on to become Miss

Minnesota. I had shared the stage with her in school musicals, and she'd collected the money from the 500 partygoers at my graduation party. Her family owned a travel agency, and I was looking to get low-cost tickets to sunny beaches for my honeymoon. When I got her on the phone, I began sharing how I was marrying one of her classmates.

"I just got married myself!" she said. "Let me tell you about where I went on my honeymoon: Medjugorje, Yugoslavia."

"You gotta be kidding me!" Then she began to tell me fantastic stories from her trip, and I knew she had no reason to pull my leg. In the years since I'd seen her, Vicki had become the polar opposite of what she and her husband had been. She had even ended up on the cover of Medjugorje Magazine. I couldn't believe it; but I did. Here she was confirming to me in her own personal experience the very things I'd read about Medjugorje. I hung up the phone, dumbfounded. I'd been seeking a cheap fare, not confirmation of Medjugorje or any spiritual advice.

Events conspired in such a way that I ended up postponing the wedding for economic reasons and instead, made plans for myself to see this Medjugorje place. One Friday in the late spring, I called Vicki. "The flights are all booked," she told me.

"Are you sure you can't find an open exit row, or something?"

"No. But if you'd like, you can try it yourself." So, after I paid my employees, I opened a fresh, cold adult beverage and began to dial. Virtually every airline I called had a seat. "Hey, Mom!" I hollered. "There are even two seats to Zurich!"

"I'll go with you!" she chirped. I asked my fiancé if she would go with us on the trip, but she declined. If you're a builder in an area of cold weather, when the frost leaves the ground in late spring, you begin to work earnestly before the ground freezes again. To go on a vacation during that time is like a farmer leaving during planting season. You just don't do it. But, knowing that within twenty-four hours, I could get a full refund for the tickets, Mom and I started to have fun with the idea and made ridiculously extravagant plans. We would go for three weeks. "Let's start off in Rome, go across the Adriatic to this Medjahoochee place, check that out, and hop over to Paris and see Sacré Coeur, Notre Dame, the gardens of Rodin, the Louvre—all sorts of Frenchee stuff."

The next morning, when I walked out to the mailbox, I reached in to find an envelope with a check for three-thousand, eight-hundred dollars from a totally unexpected source. Months earlier, I had been in a head-on collision and had to have surgery on both my knees. I noticed a billing for a surgical assistant who wasn't there and alerted the insurance company. I knew of this because I was awake during the procedure when normally patients are sedated. The insurance company didn't owe me anything. "Has it ever happened in the history of mankind," I wondered, "that an insurance company kicked a patient a big check simply for being honest?" The money would cover the entire cost of the trip. Mary had indeed paid for it.

When we arrived in Rome, we settled ourselves in a pension near the Roma Termini train station. In the morning, I called an old friend of my parents, Fr. Pung, who had met them on their honeymoon through an ordained relative of ours. Fr. Pung was now the superior of the Divine Word Missionaries, stationed at their Rome headquarters. I introduced myself and said, "We'd like to take you out to lunch while we're here."

"Oh no, oh no," he answered in a melodic Italian accent. "Give the taxi driver this address and come on over. I'm putting you up." Our cab pulled up to a stunning, wrought-iron gate, which parted majestically for us as we drove forward past saluting guards, palm trees, ornate fountains, and lush gardens. Out came our host and our "servants" to carry our bags and show us the way to our set of apartments. That entire week, drivers escorted us throughout Rome, while nuns did my laundry—nuns from Medjugorje.

The war in Yugoslavia was building up, so the U.S. state department warned travelers not to go there, and I felt perfectly fine obeying their directive. The next day the only ferry going across the Adriatic Sea would drop people off in Yugoslavia, return to Italy, and close down.

That evening, we had dinner with Fr. Pung, and he asked my mom, "Is there something I can do for you while you're still here?"

My mother answered boldly, "I'd like a relic of the True Cross."

"Good grief," I thought to myself. "Why don't you ask for clippings from Jesus' haircuts, too?"

Fr. Pung shook his head, saying, "Well, that's really hard to get. I don't know. . ." The next evening, during a goodbye dinner with him, he presented her with a relic of the True Cross from the Vatican. Mom nearly broke down and cried. We then shared with Fr. Pung that we wouldn't be going to Medjugorje because of the dangers of traveling to Yugoslavia. "Why let your faith fail you now?" he asked in reply.

I bit my tongue, thinking, "What are you talking about? Faith? This is called prudence. One does not take his sixty-two-year-old mother with a heart condition into a communist country with no way to get back out, especially when he's carrying all the bags."

But the next morning, unable to ignore his challenge, I ventured out and purchased two one-way tickets—the very last ones available for the very last boat to Yugoslavia. That evening, Mom and I found ourselves in the dining area of a car ferry, having a wonderful time partaking of Italian crusty bread, wine, and fried calamari. As we recounted the joys of our red-carpet stay in Rome, a man and two women walked up to us and sat down at our table. They introduced themselves as the DeSantos from San Diego, California. The man was married to one of the women, and the other was the wife's sister. "How are you getting up into the mountains where Medjugorje is?" they asked.

"I don't know . . . planes, trains, and automobiles?" I answered.

"No, we were called to drive you to Medjugorje."

"What!? Who 'called' you?"

"We've been over there six times," said the couple. Our daughter works for the airlines, so our airfare is free. A couple days ago, when we were home in San Diego, God told us to drive a man to Medjugorje and that we would know him when we saw him. You are that man. So we flew over here from the United States, and here we are. We are going to leave with you on this very ferry and then drive you there."

My heart almost stopped all over again. The three of them had travelled all the way from the West Coast of the United States to find me on a ferry on the East Coast of Italy, so they could drive me to Medjugorje; then they would leave Medjugorje the next day for a twenty-seven-hour journey back to San Diego.

"You've got to be kidding."

They weren't. The next morning at 6 a.m., when we arrived in Split, they rented a big car, and the five of us rode off. Driving up steep roads with no guard rails, along sheer cliffs, we proceeded on the three-hour journey to Medjugorje. Sitting uneasily in the back seat, I thought, "Six times? They've been there six times! Who goes any place on vacation six times? The town only has one paved road." When we finally saw signage for Medjugorje, my nerves erupted into a full-blown panic attack, the first and only one I've ever had. If my mother and my baggage hadn't been in the car, I would have jumped out the door and run away. The attack, I believe, was the last chance the devil had to prevent me from entering Medjugorje.

Maintaining my composure through the panic as best I could, we arrived safely in Medjugorje at noontime. We stopped at a home, about a quarter mile away from St. James Church. "Wait a minute," I said, as I looked across the town at the top of the church. "I thought the action was near St. James. Why don't we stay in a place down there?"

My mom tapped my forearm and put me gently in my place, as only a mother could do: "If you want to change dwellings tomorrow, we'll move, but I suggest you let Jesus have his way with you today." The DeSantoses had a half-day to spend there and suggested we climb Mt. Krizevac (Cross Mountain), which received its name in 1933. Medjugorje was experiencing terrible crop failure that year, so the parish priest encouraged the village do penance, erect a cement cross at the top of the mountain, and pray. They did just that, and the crops were miraculously restored.

We drove to the base of Mt. Krisevac and began to climb the rocky path up Cross Mountain, pausing at sculptured Stations of the Cross along the way. Out of breath, my mother stopped, unable to continue beyond the third or fourth station. "I just can't go any farther, but you go on, son, and I'll wait for you here." She was insistent, so I continued to climb.

When I arrived at the top of the mountain, the Lord began speaking to my heart about his original design for humanity. He had a simple plan for us to love him and love each other: he would make us in his very image, give us free will, love us as his very own, and provide all that we needed and more. In return, all he desired was that we love him back. But instead of returning the love that he continued to lavish upon the world, we gave back to him cold indifference. We profoundly altered and complicated his plan to the point that we found life a burden instead of a blessing.

Remembering my mom, I started to climb back down the mountain. Mom wasn't at the fourth station . . . the second . . . the first. When I arrived at the bottom, I found her in a small convenience store, drinking a Budvar (a Czechoslovakian Budweiser). She turned to me and asked, "How did you get down? Did you take the path or the stairs?"

"Ma, I came down the same way I went up, along the path."

"You know, son, I didn't want you to know how bad I felt and deter you from going up the mountain. I waited for you, but you were gone a long time. I didn't feel that I was steady enough to make it down the rocky path by myself, so I prayed and asked God to help me, and he showed me where the stairs were." There are no stairs on Cross Mountain. My mother was a brilliant, stable-minded woman. The reality is that such miraculous things seem like they're normal in Medjugorje.

That evening, we arrived at St. James Church an hour before Mass as the Rosary was being said. The church was jam-packed, not just standing-room-only, but like a rock concert with bodies compressed and spilling out the doors. Even with the sharpness of an Italian nun's elbow, I wouldn't have been able to burrow my way inside. (People in the know understand what I'm talking about.) So, I sat on an outdoor bench on the sunny side of the church to listen to the lilting sounds of the Rosary, coming through the loudspeaker in Croatian, followed by dozens of different languages harmonized into one voice: "Holy Mary, Mother of God, pray for us sinners now and at the hour of our death. Amen." In the middle of the Rosary, at 6:40 p.m., small church bells played "Ave Maria," announcing the arrival of the Mother of God, whom the locals affectionately call "Gospa." "So, Mary is appearing now on earth to one of the visionaries," I thought to myself. Then all went quiet, extremely quiet, and the atmosphere grew still.

People from around the globe, from Asia, Africa, Europe, and America—wearing cameras, robes, loafers, and tennis shoes, respectively—started to look up and point toward the sky. Joining them, I stood transfixed as I watched the sun shimmer and throb and shoot off beams of light. At intervals, its center turned opaque, with the outside spinning in one direction, then the other, displaying changing and swirling colors. After a few minutes, I diverted my eyes, realizing I wasn't supposed to be able to stare at the sun without going blind. I even looked for a bright spot in my vision, which naturally comes from optic fatigue. It wasn't there. Turning to the woman next to me, I asked, "Do you see that?"

"Yes, the sun is spinning!" she exclaimed, and then I learned that women describe colors differently than men. Purple, as far as I knew, could be "light purple" or "dark purple." "It's lavender!" she began. "No wait, it's turning violet, now mauve . . . actually, more like mulberry or magenta. . ." As she continued to name all the colors on a paint wheel, I thought of how I wanted to share the experience with my mom but didn't know where she was, so I began walking toward the back of the church along a pea-gravel path in search of her. At the point when I stood directly outside of where the Tabernacle resided inside the church, I was suddenly taken away . . . and shown my life.

I saw all the sinful events of my life up through the present moment. It was an illumination of conscience, an experience more intimate and vivid than a movie, more realistic than a 3-D image; and I had the sense that God was there, somewhere behind me, watching everything. I was aghast to learn the implications of my sin, how my actions or inactions were so much bigger than one single event and had a ripple effect on others across time and eternity. I didn't know that human beings were related in this way. Bawling uncontrollably, all I could say over and over again was, "I'm sorry. I'm so sorry. I didn't know." But what was clear was that in every situation, I had a choice, and I chose poorly.

The first scene God showed me was of myself as a five-year-old boy, reaching up to steal a Matchbox car, which hung from a store rack, and I felt how it broke God's heart. He loved me beyond all telling and would have given me anything. Simultaneously, God communicated the intricacies of deliberation that went into my choice. At that tender young age, I knew that taking the car was wrong. I knew my parents or my grandmother would have happily paid for it. I had no reason to steal it. God revealed to me all those things we never think of. ("It's just a toy car. What could it hurt anybody?") But my small action hurt relationships of trust. Insurance had to pay. The owner of the store had to pay. His and others' trust in their fellow human beings was further eroded, which changed their behavior—and so on, and so on. There were losses within me, as well. There was the loss of innocence. Once I performed that deed, I could never take it back. It could be confessed and forgiven, restitution might be made, but a reality would still hold that would remain part of my experience. And that could never be changed. Yet after I stole it, I didn't repent, therefore every subsequent theft became that much easier.

Then I saw, in mind-boggling detail, scenes of my moral descent into all that the world and the devil had to offer me. At first, my conscience knew that there was an undeniable selfishness attached to my transgressions because I was created and taught to know better. But as my sins grew progressively worse, my conscience became ever more muted, until in time, the voice of truth in my life was either actively ignored or shut out completely. Materialism, power, and pleasures became my gods. I saw my attachment to the forty-foot motor yacht, the big house on the river, the cool cars, the clothes, the sex, the drugs. Not once did I think of consequences because consequences didn't come to me. Without experiencing the negativity of my actions and rationalizing away any that came, I made my pursuits acceptable in my own mind. Embracing the mentality of the world today, I believed, "If they don't catch me, if they don't charge me, if they don't bring me before the magistrate, then what I'm doing is okay." God was giving me immediate and intimate knowledge of this human folly. He was exposing my cherished lies and those I embraced from society. If abortion was legal, if contraception was prescribed, didn't that make them okay? No. If state legislators legalized marijuana for everyone and called it medicinal, wasn't it always so? No, they were liars. What mattered was what God thought, what God said. But I had preferred to be ignorant of God.

I believed the damning lie that simply because two people "consent" to a sexual act, it is therefore justified. With each encounter I had with a woman, I was fully responsible for my part and partially responsible for hers. The degrees of culpability and the far-ranging, rippling repercussions were different for each act and each person. Sometimes a woman wanted to please me because she had every intention of having a deep relationship that involved marriage, and I had no intention of that whatsoever. Sometimes I had better intentions, but my sin was still sin. I could never give back what I had taken from so many women, sometimes her virginity, which was crushingly serious—worse than beating her. Even if I had run after her and told her I was sorry a thousand times, her relationships with men throughout her life would still be affected, not to mention her eternal soul. Every one of my sexual sins, like all sin, involved pain and suffering, but I hadn't allowed myself to see.

My mother wanted me to behave differently toward women, but I appeared to be cavalier and uncaring about her feelings, which wasn't the truth. In the illumination, I felt her pain within myself. She was so disappointed. Long before she moved into my home, she would visit and try her best to help me, but I continued to insist that she embrace my behavior in order to have a relationship with me. It was against her sensibilities, so she couldn't accept it, but she loved me anyway. My response was to turn my back on her physically and emotionally. "I'm not coming over to your house. I'm not seeing you!" I bellowed. This was the woman who bore me into the world, who loved me, whom God had chosen as my mother. When reliving this moment, I felt the slicing pain of rejection that had stabbed my mother's heart to its core.

Even choices that didn't seem serious to me, were, and my good intentions were never enough to cover them up. When someone passed me a joint at a rock concert, for instance, even if I didn't intend to do drugs when I was there, I still bore the responsibility for my choice to take a hit, however disinterestedly. One particular scene that bore my fingerprints was profoundly disturbing. I had sold drugs to a certain guy on more than one occasion, then moved away and never saw him again. When I returned to that area, I was sitting in a local tavern where a man told me that the guy had committed suicide. In the illumination of conscience, I was shown the event of his death. It is still so hard for me to accept and to know that in certain and real ways, I was part of his decision-making process to end his life on Earth. In seeing the ripple effects of my sin, I learned that he was holding his family together. When he died in such a way, he crushed each one of his family members. Their suffering, in turn, afflicted every relationship they had with others, and so on, in a spiral of pain.

All of the sinful events of my life passed before my eyes and through my emotions, in the eternal presence of God, where there could be no deception, no rewriting of history, no mitigation of circumstances. It was what it was. All my back stories were being erased and my guilt exposed. Like most human beings, I had rewritten the unconfessed sins of my past, creating skewed interpretations in my mind to downplay any personal culpability and disperse blame. I had decimated every one of the Ten Commandments. Intense remorse flooded my soul. I felt devastated by the heavy weight of truths about myself that I didn't want to see, didn't want to feel, didn't want to own. People had died because of my actions. I witnessed moments in my life that made me incredulous it was even me. Mortified, I just wanted to go away, to curl up and die, but I couldn't escape. I believe that had I seen the condition of my soul without the merciful support of God, I would have experienced a despair so great that I couldn't have gone on living.

When I came out of the illumination, I found myself kneeling and looking up at the miracle of the sun, still spinning and pulsating with color. Then I glanced downward to see the front of my shirt and the flagstones beneath me wet with tears. A few feet away, sitting on a bench, was my mother. I could see from her posture that she, too, could see this miracle of the sun, so I got up, walked behind her, wrapped my arms around her and rested my chin on her shoulder, cheek to cheek. Together we looked up at the most powerful energy source known to man, which God was manipulating at his discretion because he created it, and he isn't bound by the laws he made. In the presence of such a miracle, we were like little kids cuddled up in innocent awe, observing the power of God.

"How could it be," I wondered, "that scarcely any time has passed?" It then occurred to me that I had just experienced the whole of my life in the same few short minutes that Mary, the Mother of God, had appeared on Earth.

So that was my first day in Medjugorje. The next day, I woke up with an all-consuming desire to go to Confession. Donning a light jacket, I walked through the mist and rain drops, underneath scattered clouds toward St. James church. Sitting down on a wet bench, I thought to myself, "I would have liked to have gone to confession to Fr. Mike Canary"—a priest from Ireland I had met the night before, who was a late vocation. I had sensed from his demeanor that he would understand the gravity of the sins I had committed and give me a harder penance than simply five "Hail Mary's."

I didn't think of my ponderings as prayer, but no more had I finished my thought than Fr. Mike walked into my peripheral vision. For the next three hours, we sat together on that bench, huddled under his umbrella, while I told him my sins. Like St. Padre Pio, he could read into my soul; he knew the details of my sins before I said them. When I had trouble voicing my most shameful and embarrassing moments, he would help me by reminding me of particulars: ". . . and this is what you were doing . . . but this is what you were thinking . . ." When I finally finished, he gave me my penance: "You go to the mountain, the Mountain of the Cross. You take your shoes off, not as a penance, but an equalizer for all the infirm and elderly, the sick and the less able who come here. You are young and strong, and you climb that mountain in your bare feet, and you pray for every person you've ever hurt." Then he laid his hands on my head for absolution, and heat came out of them and into me. I didn't know what it was. I just knew that it was.

As I climbed the mountain, I could remember the name of every person I'd hurt. I could remember the lies, the seductions, the cheating, the thefts. I sobbed all the way to the top, and since I left my shoes at the bottom, I sobbed even more all the way down. At the base of the mountain, where a crucifix stood, I prostrated myself and begged Jesus for my life. I knew that I could walk this life perfectly from that moment on, and I would never be able to make up for all the harm I had done.

When I finally stood back up, I felt truly forgiven. I had never felt that way before in my life. I put my tennis shoes on and thanked God for his extravagant mercy. Then I walked back to the church, where I ran into Fr. Mike again. He said, "Come with me," and I followed him into a room with rows of metal folding chairs and people singing hymns. He called it a healing service. I didn't know what that meant and didn't think I necessarily needed one. I was happy because I felt forgiven. But, "What could it hurt?" Fr. Mike pulled out a purple stole, creased from being folded in his pocket, placed it around his neck, and walked to the front of the room. People stood up one at a time and walked over to him. When it came my turn, and I was standing about three feet in front of Fr. Mike, my mouth opened involuntarily, and I heard my voice say, "I have many scars on my heart, and what I want is the Holy Spirit." Putting my hand over my mouth incredulously, I thought, "Okay, that was weird. I wasn't gonna say anything."

Fr. Mike didn't utter a word. He picked up a small vial of holy oil, made the sign of the cross on my forehead, put his right hand on my head and then on my heart. All of a sudden, the Holy Spirit descended with great force, and I was afraid, not from fear, but awe. The Spirit stopped right above my heart. The experience wasn't merely psychological, physical, spiritual, or emotional, and it dwarfed any human drug or sexual sensation. What I underwent was the most explosively powerful event of my life. For those who know the original Star Trek series, I liken it to putting one's head into the "anti-matter." Fr. Mike said, "Let there be no more doubt. Let there be no more fear," and in that moment, my spirit expanded, as though taking in the biggest breath of air possible. The more I opened myself, the more he filled me, until there was no distinction between God and me. When I finally came back to consciousness of my surroundings, I found myself lying on the floor. Fr. Mike had his hand on my heart and was praying over me along with an eighteen-year-old young man named Bill Curry, who only six months earlier, had been a face-down drunk; but God delivered him from his addiction in Medjugorje.

My feet were sticking straight out and my body lay stiff, as though it had been jolted with a million volts. I could have easily served as a plank between any two of those folding chairs. Gradually, as my body began to relax, a delightful warmth I'd never known entered my soul. I had felt happiness before when winning the big game, falling in love, achieving success, and celebrating Christmas, but I'd never known what true joy really was. When I got up, I immediately embraced Fr. Mike, who said I almost broke his back I hugged him so hard. But I couldn't help it. I loved him! I loved everybody! It was sappy, and I didn't care. The experience so filled me with the Spirit of God that I could feel my heart beating with love for all of his creatures; it so cleansed my soul that I could almost feel people's bad thoughts. I walked outside into the cold outdoor air wearing a T-shirt and a smile, with no need of my sweater because I was emanating intense heat.

So that was only my second day in Medjugorje. The following day was the Feast of Corpus Christi, the Body of Christ. At dawn, as I lay in bed, I experienced another mystical event. This time, I found myself standing in a field of tall grass, about six to eight-inches high, with a wooden fence on my left, which travelled down a slope before me. A soft wind blew waves through the grass, making the underside of the blades appear silver in the sunlight. Then Jesus came. He walked up the slope in my direction and stopped a few feet in front of me, off to the left. He looked exactly like I would have expected him to. The only image I've seen that resembles his face was captured by a young artist named Akiane Kramarik,[1] a girl who could miraculously paint like a master, as a child, without any training whatsoever. She was allegedly transported to heaven and recorded on canvas what she witnessed. The face of Jesus she painted was the face that I saw. He appeared to me wearing a soft, cream-colored, inner garment flecked with brown, and over it, a dark brown outer robe with banded strands of four or five threads woven in a checkered pattern. I could clearly make out his bearded face and his intense, but inviting eyes.

Then without speaking, Jesus communicated to me, "I want you to be a priest."

I was completely taken aback. "You've got to be kidding. I am the worst sinner, ever, and we've just been through this!"

"Yes," he responded.

"But I'm engaged to be married. I love my fiancée. I've named my kids. The dress is bought. The country club is rented. Critical mass has been

---

[1] See Drawing Heaven—Akiane Kramarik, https://www.youtube.com/watch?v=md4cMFVniZY, and Heaven is for REAL Jesus Painting by Akiane Lithuania Girl Seen by Colton, https://www.youtube.cˡom/watch?v=SOX3YQMIkU

achieved. And sorry to say it, but I've been treating her like my wife already." I had never, ever, ever, ever thought of being a priest—never had a moment of altar boy fervor—no inclination—nothing—not once.

"Yes."

"C'mon. This isn't for guys like me. That's for someone else. You create those guys. You know from beyond time that they're going to be priests. You put them into a wonderful family, they come out the altar boy chute, and then—boom—they're priests."

"I know what I'm doing," he said, and then he turned and walked away.

Jesus had just laid waste to my greatest desires in life, but I couldn't deny what had just happened. Seeing Jesus was not the realization of a dream; it was the destruction of every dream I had. I felt worse than ruined. Getting out of bed, I reached over, shook my mother awake, and told her what happened. She looked me straight in the face and said, "I can't help you."

"What!?" Despondent and desperately seeking comfort, I wondered, "What do I do now?"

Not knowing where to turn, I got up and went to St. James Church for the 11 o'clock Mass. I must have been a pretty picture with my shoulder-length hair, funky mustache, and my baggy, ballooning Zubaz® pants that looked like pajama bottoms. The World Wrestling Federation had somehow gotten the NFL to wear them, and no one had been smart enough to say, "Hey, those are really ugly." My Zubaz® had red and orange flames traveling up my legs. The company's slogan is "Embrace the Awesome." I walked into the church looking like that, and a priest named Fr. Philip Pavich, who was in charge of the English-speaking Mass, asked me to do the readings.

Startled, I began to prepare, completely forgetting that I'd had a fear of public speaking. It seemed to have vanished with the old me when I was baptized in the Spirit. When I walked forward and stood behind the ambo, everything from my waist up was absolutely calm. Oddly, everything from the waist down was still shaking and knocking together, like it used to in speech class, even though I didn't feel scared anymore. The ambo hid this sorry view from the congregation, but it was in clear view of the many English-speaking priests sitting in the sanctuary. When Mass was over, I walked out of the church past the door to the sacristy to join my mother

OF MEN AND MARY

and a woman named Lynn. "Mom," I said, "wasn't that really cool that I did the readings?"

She said, "I was behind a pillar. That wasn't your voice."

Then, as the thirty-seven priests who were on the altar left the sacristy, they walked up to the three of us, one after the other. They had to have seen me proclaiming the Word of God with my flaming Zubaz®, my wavy, long hair, my groovy mustache, and my reverberating knees, yet every single one of them asked me, "Are you a priest?"

"No," I responded to each one. "I'm engaged to be married." But no matter my response, each would reply, "We need you," and then turn and walk away. Every single priest said the exact same words to me. My mother and Lynn and I began to find this equally astounding as amusing.

One English-speaking cleric visiting Medjugorje, who was the chaplain for Lynn's pilgrimage group, was missing. "You should talk to him," Lynn urged. He's a great priest." I thought perhaps he might be able offer some consolation; but the day passed, and I couldn't find him.

Night came, and with it, the loss of hope that I would find any relief from my inner torment. As I sat next to the statue of Our Lady that adorns the front courtyard of St. James Church, I sighed, "Give me a sign, Lord, please—some kind of consolation. Help me!" Then I looked up at the sky and saw a green beam of light, like a meteorite, hit the large cross atop Cross Mountain; and at the moment of impact, it appeared to burst into flame. That cross, made of nothing but cement, began to "burn." But the miracle didn't make me feel one bit better. A few minutes later, the priest walked up. Relieved, I said that I wanted to speak with him, so we walked side-by-side through a cemetery in the direction of Cross Mountain. As I poured out my soul, he started to laugh. "Hey, I'm being serious here," I said to him, which only made him laugh all the more.

"What do you think I do at home?" he asked.

I paused to think for a moment. "You're not in vocations to the priesthood, are you?"

"Yep." I felt like the joke was on me, and I wasn't finding it at all funny. We came to a fork in the dirt road: one direction led to Mt. Krisevac, the other to Podbrdo. "It is said that the Hill of the Apparitions is the spiritual path, and Cross Mountain is the path of the world," he said. "Our mission is to bring those two mountains together in our lives." And then he took his leave of me. I stood there alone at the crossroads, inconsolable.

As night fell, I turned and walked toward the Hill of the Apparitions. In the ambient light of the moon, I began to climb, looking for any kind of human consolation. A man came toward me, carrying a flashlight. I engaged him with small talk and said, "I'll follow behind you." But following his flashlight seemed more difficult than climbing under the moonlight. He ended up getting us profoundly lost. I was feeling a bit perturbed when I heard a small voice within me say, "I made you to lead, not to follow." So I took leave of him and walked only twenty to thirty feet to find myself at the sight of the first apparition of the Mother of God. Sitting down on a comfortable rock, I stared out over the town. Bright flames of orange and yellow were still "consuming" the cement cross atop Mt. Krisevac, and it remained on "fire" throughout the entire night. As midnight approached, I heard something that I never had before. The birds began to sing—not chirp or call, but sing, like canaries, with more and more of them blending their voices together across the whole valley. It was beautiful, incredibly beautiful. And yet it didn't comfort me. I simply sat on the hill and cried.

After spending a week in Medjugorje, my mother didn't want to leave and suggested that we set up a shop and sell religious souvenirs, staying there for the rest of our lives. But Our Lady tells the pilgrims through the visionaries that we need to come down off the mountain, go home to our people, and tell them about the love of God. For the very first time, I wasn't looking forward to seeing my fiancée. In fact, I was dreading it. When the plane landed, I felt my stomach twist into a knot. "Welcome home, honey!" she exclaimed at the airport with open arms. I knew what those open arms would lead to, and I also knew I had to somehow avoid them.

"I'm tired," was the excuse I repeated for a few days. When Sunday came, she and my mother and I went to Mass and stopped afterward at a Farm and Fleet store. While we were standing in the checkout line, a guy in front of me, whom I knew from daily Mass, turned around to say, "So, when are you going to go talk to the bishop about priesthood?"

My fiancée's head snapped around so fast I thought she'd get whiplash. It would be a long ride home and the beginning of the end of our relationship. I never dated again, and in a certain way, I've never stopped loving her. She was a good woman, and she married a few years later. Unsurprisingly, I wasn't invited to the wedding. I still pray for her and hope she found love with someone who brought her joy and children.

When I approached the diocese in which I lived and told the vocation director, who was several years my junior, my entire fantastic story, he looked at me with a puzzled and anxious expression and advised me to go home and pray about it for a year. I thought to myself, "Aren't I supposed to discern the priesthood while in the seminary and not only before?"

I continued to attend Mass every day, and when I saw members of the Rosary group, I told them the details of my Medjugorje trip. All of them believed my hard-to-swallow story, probably because I had no reason to lie. After daily Mass, I began to lead the Rosary, and people enjoyed the way I would extemporaneously describe the mysteries. Soon, I was invited to other prayer groups to do the same. Meanwhile, interest in my conversion story was growing.

After about four months, I was asked to lead the Rosary for a day-long conference, which drew about 800 people, and during the conference, the organizers spontaneously asked me if I would tell the story of my conversion. I agreed, and when I stepped up to the podium, again, every trace of fear left me. I spoke of God's love and mercy in my life, of how the dead will rise and proclaim the glory of God. Glancing down past the front of the stage, I could see the nationally known speakers of the conference staring up at me, captivated. Looking out into the crowd I could see the presence of the Holy Spirit wash over the listeners. I had not planned what I was going to say. The story came out more beautifully than I could ever have told it myself, and when I was finished, people sat in their seats, stunned; then they stood up and started an ovation that lasted for what seemed to me like too long. "How could this be?" I wondered. "What did I say that they enjoyed? I was just telling them about a lousy sinner who received God's mercy, and of how the Mother of God had called me to Medjugorje that I might better know the love of the Father and the Son and the Holy Spirit. I hadn't even mentioned my call to the priesthood. That I kept very close to myself.

That year, I began to travel across dioceses in other states to share my story, and the Lord used me to organize a Marian conference at the St. Paul Civic Center in Minnesota, which drew nearly 10,000 attendees. "Who is this long-haired guy with too much facial hair and no fashion sense?" people wondered. In time, a radio interview I gave was picked up by the Catholic Digest and printed.

Fall turned to winter, and winter to spring. As I was getting ready for Mass one Sunday morning, the phone rang. My mother said it was for me.

"Mom, take a message!" I called out from another room. "Otherwise, we're going to be late for Mass."

"It's a bishop," she responded. "I suggest you take the call."

"Hello?"

On the other end of the line, a gentle voice said, "I am Bishop James Sullivan of the diocese of Fargo, North Dakota. I just read an article about you, and I believe you have a vocation to be a priest. I want you to come to my diocese and stay with me and talk with me." I fell speechless. That information was only between God and me. I don't know what I finally mumbled—something like, "I'll think about it, and I should go to church now."

I decided to travel to his diocese, just to speak with him and attend a local shooting tournament. But the kindly Bishop Sullivan asked when I was with him, "Would you please go and talk to the rector of the seminary? Please do it for me."

I said, "Okay, Bishop, but I am not going to enter the seminary. I simply came here to talk to you." So I went over to the minor seminary where I was welcomed by a group of priests. They invited me to sit down with them in a conference room, where I shared my incredible story of Jesus asking me to be a priest. They laughed and they laughed and they laughed. There it was again. "I'm serious." I told them.

"Don't worry," they said, "the bishop has told us we can't throw you out, no matter how crazy you sound." Suddenly, we heard a knock on the door. As it opened, I saw standing before me my good friend, Mike, from Wisconsin, all 6 feet 5 inches, 330 pounds of him. I had met big Mike a year earlier on a return trip to Medjugorje, where we bonded in the knowledge that one day we both had to enter the seminary. His story was similar to mine. He was recruited by the Cleveland Browns—a fulfillment of his life-long dream of becoming a professional football player, when the Lord called him in Medjugorje to the priesthood. Unbeknownst to me, the bishop had tracked him down, too. Mike walked forward and threw his arms around me, dwarfing my 5-foot 10-inch, 250-pound frame. "You know this guy?" exclaimed the priests.

Bishop Sullivan, a humble man, guided by the hand of God and moved by his profound relationship with the Blessed Mother, would pave the way for me to become a priest. Neither Mike nor I ever filled out an application or provided transcripts to the seminary. The bishop accepted us, protected us, and loved us. I arrived in Fargo with three pairs of dirty jeans, four different shotguns, seven cases of shells, one little, yellow lab named Sugar, and zero intention of staying. In the seminary, where there was a rule against pets, Sugar lived openly in my room for the next two years and ended up in every official picture taken.

My time at the seminary in Fargo turned out to be a blessed springboard for my eventual return to my home diocese of Milwaukee, Wisconsin, where I would be ordained and where I would tend to my mother until the day she died on October 24, 2016. In her last conscious moments, as I sat by her bedside, I couldn't help but shower my mom with my love. I kept kissing her through my tears and thanking her for bringing me into life, for being such a great mom, and for loving me out of hell. As I drove home from her place of care, I lifted up my hands to heaven, praised God for her life, and said to him, "You gave me your mom on the Cross, and now I give my mom back to you. Please come and take her to yourself." That very night, she went peacefully to the Lord.

There exists an ancient belief that when a priest's mother dies, at the moment she reaches heaven, she gives to Jesus a cloth with the sacred chrism oil that anointed her son's hands for ministry and says, "I gave you a priest, my son." When I attended my mother's funeral, pains of love and sorrow and gratitude and loss overwhelmed me as I imagined this encounter between them, and I bowed my head and cried, like a small child. Now I await that joyful day outside of time when I will join her, when I will hear all about the reception she received in heaven, because I don't just believe that God exists. I know that He exists.

THREE

JIM JENNINGS

A Murderer Changes His Eternal Life Sentence

I'M AN EX-CONVICT. I've spent eighteen of the last twenty-five years in prison. My charges consisted of murder, attempted murder in the first degree, atrocious assault and battery, attempted murder of a police officer, armed robbery and escape. And there are a lot of things I never got caught for. But I believe in my heart that my attitude toward life was my worst sin. I didn't at all like myself, and if I didn't care for myself, I surely wasn't gonna care about you—about hittin' you in the head or takin' what you had from your pocket. I was on a self-destruction trip with an attitude that wounded my mind and my soul. I've been a drug addict and an alcoholic; I've abused sex and satiated myself with every vice imaginable. If I was tempted to do it, I did it.

When I was first charged with murder in 1970, my home state of New Jersey tried to give me the electric chair, but the jury acquitted me of first- and second-degree murder and found me guilty of manslaughter. I got twenty to thirty years for that, but after eight years, I was paroled. After stayin' out six years, I got locked up again in Tennessee 'cause of new charges for attempted murder and only got fifteen that time. They were lookin' to give me three twenty-fives to life. I was lucky. I would've never seen daylight.

In 1984, I went back to prison, my fourth time in, for three counts of attempted murder in the first degree. In 1988, I finally got parole from Tennessee State Prison. I still had a possible detainer from New Jersey and knew I could end up there with ninety days for parole violation, but come June, I was goin' home. I'm a carpenter—a good one, and I had plans of goin' out into the world and makin' a lot of money. Even though I've stolen a lot in my life, I'd rather work for a livin'; and since I've got a bad temper and been in subcultures where violence comes about, I figured I'd avoid all that and stay out of jail. But I was gonna live life the way I knew how to live it—in vice. My plan was to dedicate the rest of my days to my own pleasures. The last thing on my mind was God.

In early May of 1988, the prison called an evening headcount, which is when the prisoners stay locked in their cells for half an hour while the guards make sure everybody is accounted for. After the officer walked by, me and my cell partner rolled up a couple of joints and got high. Meanwhile, I turned on the TV to the public broadcasting station 'cause I like animal shows and stuff like that. Well, they had somethin' on there about the Blessed Virgin Mary. They showed these six kids lookin' up and speakin' in a foreign language, while the narrator starts talkin' about the Mother of God. Lookin' at those kids faces, I just knew it was real. I had years of experience sniffin' out phonies, and I knew they weren't makin' that up. They were really seein' Our Lady! And that's the moment my life started to change.

I turn to my cell partner and says, "What do ya think of that?"

"What?" he says.

"They say the Blessed Virgin Mary's appearing some place. The narrator was sayin' it."

He looks at me and says, "Who's the Blessed Virgin Mary?" I laughed at him and figured he was dumb as a box of rocks. Everybody knew her. Then I forgot all about it. A week or so passed, and one day around 9 in the morning, I walked outside in the Tennessee State Prison into bright blue skies and warm air. It was a beautiful Saturday morning I'll never forget. You could see all the way into Missouri across the Mississippi river. I was walkin' around in circles with a friend 'cause that's all you can do in a prison yard. We weren't talkin' or anything, just strollin'.

All of a sudden, this pressure came over me, in me, and around me, and it just kept gettin' more intense, scaring me to death. I thought I had finally crossed the line. I'd gone nuts. I wanted to run, just physically run away, out of my skin, but I couldn't. I could only walk forward. From the outside, it seemed like I was doin' exactly what I'd been doin' a few seconds earlier, but I wasn't. I wanted to talk to the guy next to me, figurin' if I did, maybe I could get my mind off of this pressure. But I couldn't even talk. I was stuck in a forward motion with my focus forced into what was happenin' in that moment.

Suddenly, I knew there was a God. I had no doubt of his existence, just like I know that I exist. At the same time, I understood the reality of heaven and hell. I didn't see nothin' with my eyes; I just suddenly knew these things. Heaven was peace and love and happiness and all the things we hear about heaven being, and hell was an eternal suffering. I mean it was ugly, and there ain't no parole. You're there for the duration.

Then I saw myself in the light of God's justice. I was standin' on the brink of hell, and it terrified me. I understood that I had a choice to make. Heaven and hell were before me, so to speak, and in my fear, I grabbed heaven sayin', "Yeah, yeah, I'll take that," thinkin' I was doin' the right thing. But I felt pushed away when I reached for it, and that freaked me out even more. Not givin' up, I tried again and said, "Yeah, I want that. I'll take heaven." But again, I was repelled from this choice. What I understand now, but didn't understand then, was that I wasn't making a real choice for heaven. In my understanding, there was a road goin' to heaven and another goin' to hell, and I was tryin' to bend the road that leads to hell to make it wind up in heaven. So, no wonder I was bein' repelled. That don't work.

I guess God felt sorry for me because all of a sudden, I got clarity within this pressure—like a sense of him tellin' me, "You have a choice to make that is entirely yours. You don't have to pick heaven. You don't have to pick hell. I'm not gonna bop you on the head and force you either way. But you must pick one or the other." Then I knew that if I continued embracing this road to hell, which was my life, I also had to embrace that end, that consequence, which was eternal suffering. But if I wanted heaven, I had to relinquish the road I was on and embrace all that would bring me to heaven.

Then I sort of seen my soul. I was able to look down inside of myself at all the things in my life I held dear. One at a time, each of my treasures, my gods, my idols—all my attachments showed up before my eyes, so to speak, and I had to let each and every one of them go. My total abandonment to these sins had to be stopped through a deliberate choice, so I said in my head, "All right. Well, okay, I'll let that go. I'll be good." "Yeah, I'll never do that again . . . or that again." This seemed to cut my sins at the root. It felt like I was goin' into the bottom of a big trash bin as the garbage was turned loose. In my state of mind, it was easy to do because I felt scared to death. When I'd finally cleaned everything out, I thought, "Yeah, I want heaven, but I don't know how to get there."

With that, the pressure eased off of me, and I was back in control again. Dazed and confused, I started walkin' away from my friend to be alone in my cell. When I got there, I couldn't do nothin'. I just sat there awestruck. I mean this rocked me. I'd never even thought about anything like this. With all the drugs I'd used, I didn't think I could ever get that high to have somethin' like that happen to me.

I started starin' at a rosary a priest had given me when I first went to prison in Tennessee. It had been hangin' there on my cell wall for about four years—who knows why; and it was just a mess with so much grease and fuzz hangin' from it that it looked like a poorly decorated Christmas tree. I'd never had a devotion to Our Lady and had said the Rosary maybe two or three times in my life, when I'd gone to Catholic school in my earlier grades, but somehow, I remembered parts of it. I didn't get religious right away, but I started thinkin' about God and tried to pray.

Over the next couple days, this peace comes over me, and I start to think about God. Then about a week after my incident happened, a guy comes runnin' up to me, who wasn't even one of my buddies, and he says, "Hey, Jim, you Catholic? There's a priest comin' here on Thursdays, and he's gonna say Mass."

Now, I was in West Tennessee—the Bible Belt. The only thing they had goin' on were Protestants comin' in and tryin' to evangelize people, and I didn't want to hear anything about anything. I didn't care if they was a priest, or a minister, or what. But all the time I'd been in this prison, I'd never seen a Catholic priest or a Catholic service. Even if they'd had them, I wasn't gonna go, but still, I didn't see none.

That Thursday, for the first time, I went down to Mass and to Confession, which I thought was a pretty good idea in light of everything that had happened. I had given away the few drugs I had left and said I wasn't dealin' no more. My friends thought I was crazy. Then every Thursday for the rest of my time there, I went to Confession and received the Eucharist until June 29, 1988, when I got picked up and transported back to New Jersey. It turned out they did want me.

For nine days, I was in transit. An eighteen-hour trip takes nine days when you're in a prison transport van. Travelin' all over the country, handcuffed, shackled, and belted down, all I could do was pray, look at the trees goin' by, and think about what had happened to me. At least, I'm pretty sure I was prayin' because the guy was goin' about 100 miles per hour. I was strapped down—couldn't even put my hands up to protect myself—and afraid of goin' right through the steel mesh in front of me. So when I got to the state prison, I was a little more devout.

In New Jersey, there were five prisons on this one big acreage, like a big prison farm. They quit growin' vegetables, and now they're just growin' prisons. Instead of the ninety days I was expectin', they wanted me to max out. I would be there another two and a half years. A Catholic priest named Fr. Hewett was on the grounds, if you could catch him runnin' through those five prisons each day. It made all the difference that he was there.

At this point, I was goin' to Mass and doin' a lot of things I figured God wanted me to do, but I didn't see my experience with God as a gift of mercy. I didn't see it as love. I'd been happily goin' off to hell, and he came in unannounced and threw a monkey wrench in the deal. Now I was scared to death of goin' off to hell, figurin' I was goin' there anyway.

So I served God for the next six to eight months in complete fear to the point of anxiety attacks. You can't imagine how scared I was. God was a giant cop up there in heaven just waitin' for me to mess up. I used to catch the priest whenever he came to the prison and make him hear my confession, and when I left the confessional, I'd wanna run right back in. If I wasn't Godlike from the second I walked out—"Oh no, here come the lightning bolts."

Everything I was doin'—prayin', Mass, goin' to Confession, sayin' a zillion Rosaries—was so that maybe, maybe, God would keep hell off of me. Fr. Hewett, the priest chaplain, told me casually, one day, to pray all the time. He probably meant that I could offer my work up as a prayer, or somethin'. Me, I start sayin' Hail Mary's at my prison carpentry job. All through the day, I was bangin' my fingers, tryin' to hammer nails while takin' papers out of my pocket to read the Hail Holy Queen. I wasn't gettin' any work done.

Then one Saturday they announced over the intercom: "Catholic Queen of Peace group is now meeting in the multi-purpose room."

"I ain't never heard of nothin' like that," I says. But it sounded like something extra I could do. I went into this room where there were four inmates, a bunch of little old ladies, a mound of Rosary beads, and some cookies. The guys who showed up were a bunch of rocket ships—I mean, real nuts. One of them had a beanie on his head and was talkin' about fruits and vegetables. He didn't know if he was Jewish, Muslim, Baptist, Catholic, or what. Another guy, obviously Protestant, was sayin' how Catholics were gonna go to hell. Then there was a Protestant becomin'

Catholic, and a Catholic who never came to Mass. So I figured, naturally, "These guys are here for the cookies."

At the end of my first time with the Catholic Queen of Peace group, one of the little old ladies pushed a newsletter toward me, called *The Miracle of Medjugorje* by Wayne Weible. These ladies had their own box of prayers, song books, little Rosary materials, Legion of Mary literature—all sorts of holy stuff that they brought in there to save us poor inmates, and they didn't especially want this newsletter in their box, so they just slid it over to me. Why I picked it up, I don't know, but I brought it back to my unit. Well, I didn't believe what it was sayin'. I didn't believe that the Virgin Mary was appearing to some six kids in Medjugorje. But there was a couple things that sounded Catholic enough, so I did them: seven Our Father's, seven Hail Mary's, seven Glory Be's, and the whole Rosary—all fifteen decades at a time. Mary supposedly said to fast on Fridays, so I started fasting one day a week on bread and water. I didn't know she wanted Wednesdays, too, otherwise I'm sure I woulda done that also because it was more stuff I could do to show God, "Hey, look! See! I'm tryin'. Hold onto that lightning bolt."

Two things in the article baffled me, though. The Virgin Mary said, "Pray with your heart," and "Love the love that's in your heart." By this point, I'm sayin' 15,000 Hail Mary's a day but still scared to death, serving God in abject fear. I didn't know what it was to love or be loved.

I'd walk around the compound with my hands in my pockets so that nobody could see me prayin' the Rosary. And bein' that I was a respectable convict, I didn't do nothin' to show any kind of weakness. I'd been wild, involved in strikes, riots, and stabbings. And now I'm tryin' to love the love that's in my heart. "What do you mean?" I'd ask Mary, afraid to ask someone else, in case they thought I was crazy. "Ah, I'm probably just nuts," I'd say to myself. "That encounter with God really didn't happen." But it happened enough to make me not dare to think it didn't happen.

One night I was out prayin', asking Mary the same question, like I asked her every night: "How do you pray with your heart?" when suddenly the world seemed to stop. Everything got quiet, and I could see real clear. I looked around at these guys walkin' around in prison involved with chasing this, chasing that, doing this and doing that—but with nothin'. They reminded me of walkin' dead people, zombies. I'm not a cryin' type person, but I was in tears, begging for each one of them. Us guys in prison don't grow up and say, "Well, I think I want to spend the rest of my life behind bars." The path there usually starts from hurt or pain. Something went terribly wrong somewhere in our lives, and we perpetuated our own hardness, over and over again, the further we got away from grace. It broke my heart that they didn't know why they was alive, and I felt that they didn't want to hear about why, so it was hard to say anything to any of 'em about God.

I guess that's how Our Lady was tryin' to teach me to pray with my heart. Feelin' sorry for them, I started prayin', "For this one, for that one . . . and I says, "Why don't you do somethin' to these guys? Why don't you do to them what you did to me? Why don't you zap 'em? Why don't you make them know you're there?"

And then I noticed . . . it wasn't only the guys in the prison, but the guards. If God wasn't the center of their being, they looked dead. And that really rocked me. It affected me real bad, so I tried to pray more and sacrifice more. I started adding fasting on Mondays and feast days, as well as on Wednesdays and Fridays, so I was really pushin' it. Some days, when I was really hungry, I'd want to give in and have chicken, or cake, or somethin' they served in the prison, but I started to understand that I could give it up for love. "I'll suffer that pain in my stomach for that person," I says to myself. And when I got tempted to change my mind and say, "Ah, I'm weak, I need to eat this," somethin' else in me would say, "Maybe I won't." You just learn how to do stuff like that. Our Lady was workin' in my heart without me even knowin' it.

Well, a couple months of this went by, and I walked over to Mass one day where Fr. Hewett had a stack of them newsletters. That's probably where them little old ladies got 'em from. Fr. Hewett don't push nothin'. This guy, he just lets the Holy Spirit work. So after Mass, he says, "I've got some of these newsletters if anybody wants them." It was the same newsletter about Medjugorje that I'd already read. Well, I go up and grab one. Now what possessed me to do that, I don't know. I don't ever read anything twice, especially somethin' I don't believe. But I brought the newsletter back to the dormitory and read it again. This time, it grabbed me. It touched somethin' inside.

So I got curious and started readin' that paper over and over. The way the kids described Mary was so beautiful. She just oozed love. When it came to Jesus, I'd heard talk of how he loved me and stuff, and I believed he died for me, but I didn't really get it. My thinkin' was, "God loves us, and well, maybe if I'm next to decent people, he won't zap me because he might take out some of them, too, by mistake." But if they weren't nearby, I was in trouble. I'd never heard of Our Lady zappin' nobody, though. You know what I mean? She's Mom.

Our Lady would always invite the six kids from Medjugorje to pray, and she'd smile at them and tell them to wear a coat and somethin' warm on their legs the next day because it would be cold. She was just love. When they described her beautiful blue eyes, I thought, "Man, I wish I could see those eyes." I didn't care if they were yellow, purple, or striped, as long as they were her eyes. I wanted them to just pierce me, to cut right through all the garbage that was inside of me, so I could open up and try to love God or somethin'.

Well, somethin' in me got stimulated. I went over to Father and says, "Hey Father, what do you think about this Blessed Virgin Mary appearing over there in Medjugorje?"

Fr. Hewett don't get moved by every little thing. He's a regular knock-around guy, so I figured his advice was trustworthy. He said, "Well, I can't speak for the Church because whatever they say goes, and they haven't said anything one way or another, but the good thing about it is they haven't condemned it. I was over in Medjugorje. I heard confessions, saw some pretty profound conversions, and noticed a great sense of peace. Personally, I think that Our Lady is there. As a matter of fact, I'm going again next week."

I said, "Oh, yeah?" And I left. As I'm walkin' around thinkin' about what he said, I start wonderin' if I can get some kind of extra holy zap, maybe send somethin' over there to get blessed. I wanted a healing like people get from water from Lourdes, France—some kind of somethin' to help me understand that Mary loved me, too, that the things she was sayin' to those kids, she was sayin' to me, too. If I could only believe this kind of stuff, believe that I'm loved, that God loves me.

Then I remembered I had a scapular. My mom had sent it to me in the mail when I lived in Florida about seven or eight years earlier. Mom was always real religious, and while I thank her now, it seemed like she was always tryin' to shove this kinda stuff down my throat. But I was glad for this scapular; it was cloth, not one of them paper ones, and it had the words, "Whosoever dies wearing this scapular shall not suffer eternal fire." That sounded pretty good, but when the scapular came, I was livin' in adultery with a woman. I put it right on, and that same night it broke. Maybe it didn't like my situation. Figurin' it was still good to have, I wrapped up the scapular, tied the strings in a knot, and carried that thing in my pocket for about eight years, even in prison.

So I reached into my pocket and pulled out this scapular, now with about six pounds of lint attached to it. After cleanin' it, I went to Fr. Hewett and said, "Look, why don't you take this over to Medjugorje with you?"

He said, "Ah, Jim. You don't understand. At customs they give you a hard time, and I might lose it."

But I said, "No, come on. Come on, Father. Give it to Marija. The newsletter says Marija is real spiritual, ya know. Give it to Marija to hold, and maybe Our Lady will get somethin' from God to give to me on this scapular."

He said, "Jim, you can't even get next to these seers because there are hundreds, sometimes thousands, of people surrounding them.

"Come on, take it anyway, Father. Try."

"All right. Everything over there is blessed by Our Lady, anyway, because she's there."

So he took my scapular over to Medjugorje. In the meantime, while I'm waitin' for him to come back, I found a scapular investment prayer for the priest to say and a morning offering I could pray in order to live out the scapular stuff—all from the box the little old ladies brought in. I'm figurin' I'm gonna do this good, ya' know. Well, he comes back, and he did get next to one of the seers, Vicka. He put the scapular in her hand, and then he had to run her down because I guess she thought it was a gift or somethin'—this broken-looking all balled-up thing.

I sewed the scapular where the string was broke, took it to Confession and Mass, and says, "Hey, Father, come on. Invest me with this scapular will you? And bless it first." My mother wouldn't have sent me nothin' that wasn't blessed, but I didn't think of that then.

He said, "It's probably blessed already. Did you make your first Holy Communion in a Catholic school? If so, you probably were invested in it then."

I says, "I don't know if I was or wasn't." So we started arguing back and forth. He's Irish, just like me. Finally, he does it. He invests me with the scapular.

That week, all of a sudden, I received such a gift of faith. When I read the Bible, it would speak to me. Before that, I had a hard time reading the Gospels and couldn't believe that Jesus was doin' all those things. Now I believed. And a love for Our Lady seemed to blossom and grow inside of me. I just wanted to do everything for her.

My whole life I never knew how to love. I wasn't the toughest person in the world, but I was willing to hurt somebody before they hurt me, and I projected that. In the prison, some guys, they've got this face that looks like you just wanna take it right off the front of their head. I mean, they just got an attitude, ya know what I mean? And they do things . . . well, prison ain't a holy place, ya know? People step in front of you when there's a line, which is dumb because if you get mad, you can just choke 'em. I had a real bad temper, and one guy got on my nerves. Every time I seen this guy, all I wanted to do was hit him.

One day after the scapular thing, I seen him, and he was cuttin' up in the line askin' for some cake, and other guys were sayin', "Hey you ain't gettin' nothin'," but with words that weren't so nice.

Then I said, "Hey, you want mine?" And I'm thinkin', "What possessed me to say that? Because if I give it to him, I'm gonna smash it into his face."

"What, you don't want it?" he says.

I says, "Nah, you can have it," and he took it.

When I did that for Our Lady, all that tension between him and me just eased. He even acted different around me, and when I seen him after that, I started thinkin' of him as a human being havin' the same problems that got me where I was at.

Our Lady kept on givin' me this desire to love her. I wanted to do all kinds of things for her. There were some goofy things I did, too. I read about the kids in Fatima, how Jacinta and them was mortifying their senses and all that kinda stuff. And these kids suffered. I mean they really suffered, voluntarily, for poor sinners. When they played, they'd get these leaves with stickers and make 'em pop in their hands, and if they got stuck, they'd offer that up. Jacinta had a little rope she tied around her, and from the day she put it on, it had blood stains all over it. These little kids was doin' that kinda stuff, and I felt like a real heel. I wanted to do more stuff for Our Lady, so when I heard about a hair shirt, I went down to the carpenter shop where I worked in the prison. We had this radial arm saw with big teeth in it, and when it cut through the wood, it didn't put out sawdust; it produced long thin splinters. When nobody was lookin', I'd take a handful of splinters and put 'em all down my shirt. So now I had a hair shirt. And I'd stand there with my arms stickin' out, like a little kid bundled up for snow. I was the lead carpenter who had to handle most of the major construction they had at the prison, and I'd try to go to work, but I couldn't move.

So I went to the priest one day and asked him if it was all right to mortify my senses. He asked me what I was doin' and did it make me feel uncharitable to people. I says, "No, I just offer all this stuff up, ya know?" Then he asked if I could do my work, and I says, "No, not really. You can't move around with all them splinters stickin' in you." He advised I cut it out. What a relief.

And then Father brought me a book called *The Queen of Peace Visits Medjugorje* by Fr. Joseph Pelletier. I opened this book, and when I seen pictures of these kids lookin' up at somethin', it just went through me; there was no doubt in my mind that those kids were seein' somethin' real, just by the looks on their faces. I had to put the book down and take a deep breath. "Wow," I thought. "Not only does God really exist, but he loves us." That's what got me. "He LOVES us. US!—right here and now, and he's lettin' us know by sending us the Blessed Virgin Mary." That thought went all over me and through me and made my hair stand up. I ate that book up. I was really on fire. For a month, as a matter of fact, I was hoping and expecting Mary would appear above the prison. I walked around lookin' up and got a stiff neck. I wanted it so bad.

But I didn't know how to get the word out about God. I'd get somebody to show up to the Rosary group every once in a while, but they wouldn't come back. In fact, they would avoid me when they seen me on Saturday—"Time for the Queen of Peace prayer group." My friends knew I was really out of character and thought I was nuts.

Meanwhile, I was growing in love for God through what Our Lady was doin', and I was prayin' hard to learn to love Jesus with all my heart, like he deserved to be loved. I wanted to serve him without fear and to understand his love more deeply in my soul so that I could say, even when I messed up, "I believe that you love me." I searched through a bunch of novenas and found one to St. Joseph. He's a carpenter, and so am I, so I figured I'd ask for his help. I started prayin' to him that day, and when I counted out the nine days for the novena, I saw that it would end on the "Feast of St. Joseph, Husband of Mary." "Wow!" I thought. "What a coincidence."

St. Joseph's feast day was on a Saturday, so that day I went over to the Rosary group with the little old ladies. This other volunteer, a young fella named Bob comes in with a little bag of books and says, "Here. My neighbor sent these in." Usually, this neighbor sent in stuff like Mass bulletins from 1939, but I grabbed the bag 'cause I was readin' whatever I could. The first book I pulled out was a little black one called *The Secrets of Mary* by St. Louis de Montfort. All I seen was some "thee's" and "thou's," so I put that old archaic English right down. Well, this book, it drew me. I kept wantin' to pick it up; then I'd put it down; then I'd pick it up, again. There was like a magnet on it.

I went back to the dormitory at "count time" when everybody is present, and again, this little black book draws me to it sayin', "READ ME!" Finally, I says, "Man, what is this thing?" I open it up and start to read, and on the first page of the first chapter, it said, "The Secrets of Mary and the doctrine of the slavery of Love." Somehow, I knew with my whole heart that St. Joseph had come through for me. In my little pea brain, I didn't understand it, but my soul just leapt. My hair was standin' on end. It continued, "Predestinate soul, I am about to share with you a secret that the Most High has taught me that I have been unable to find in any book written anywhere." I said, "Wow!" Those words just went all through me. I didn't even know what he was talkin' about. I had no idea this was about a consecration to Mary, or even what a consecration was, but my soul knew because my whole body was on fire. Even now when I think about it, my hair stands straight up.

A little further on in the book, St. Louis de Montfort said somethin' like, "Before you get carried away, get on your knees and say the Veni Creator Blest and the Ave Maris Stella." I'd never heard of these prayers, but I looked in the back of the book and found 'em. I'm not an emotional person, but this moved me. All around me, there's people in the dormitory, and now he's askin' me to get on my knees in front of everybody. I ain't never got on my knees to pray in front of nobody, but I wasn't gonna blow this. St. Louis said, "Get on your knees," so I got on my knees. Tryin' hard to see the words while wiping my eyes from cryin', I managed to say the prayers.

After I read *The Secrets of Mary*, consecrating myself to her was now the most important thing in my life, but I didn't know how to. I wanted to make this consecration immediately. I mean NOW, yesterday! To me, it was like becomin' ordained a priest or somethin'. I wanted to give my life to Our Lady—especially in light of the faith God had given me through the grace of Our Lady of Medjugorje. I wanted to belong to her and give myself totally to Jesus through her.

The next Saturday, which happened to be Holy Saturday, a lady in the prayer group who had no idea about the consecration says to me, "Here, Jim," and gives me this little orange book called, *Preparation for Total Consecration to Jesus through Mary According to St. Louis de Montfort*, a thirty-three-day preparation for consecration to Our Lady. "That's really remarkable," I says. "This is just what I needed." The front of the book had a little calendar listing a few days in the year when you could start the consecration, and the next date was the very next day, March 26, Easter Sunday. Really pumped, I started the thirty-three days of prayer on Easter and was consecrated on April 28th, the Feast Day of St. Louis de Montfort. I figured God was workin' overtime.

Now I had to live this consecration because on the last day of preparation, my penance from Fr. Hewett was: "Live the consecration for the rest of your life." There was no turning back. I had to trust in Our Lady because I really didn't feel like I was worthy to be one of hers, let alone anything of hers; but I wanted it so bad. Believe me, I was havin' a rough time being good and still had to go to Confession every time I turned around, but I would do the little things that I could to please Our Lady. When I was ready to run my mouth at somebody, I'd let her have my mouth; and she wouldn't do that stuff, so automatically I'd clam up. If one of the women in the prison was walkin' by, and I was lookin' at her too hard, I gave Our Lady my eyes. If I didn't look at her with love, I mean a real love—of her soul and stuff, I wouldn't look at her.

This was a gift from God 'cause I didn't even know how to love, but I was excited to do things for Mary since she was so wonderful. And then things started to happen around me. I started to go up to guys and say, "Hey, there's a few of us gettin' together to have this prayer group, and we're gonna live according to these messages of Medjugorje," and I'd toss them one of the Wayne Weible newsletters. But there wasn't no "few" of "us." There was just me. I thought maybe people would come if I added numbers. Good thing they didn't ask me who.

I went to the priest and said, "Hey Father, how about if we get a prayer group together and start livin' these messages of Medjugorje?"

He said, "Jim, forget it. I've been tryin' to get a prayer group going for eight years and couldn't do it. The institution isn't going to give you a room, and even if they did, I'd have to be there, and I can't with five prisons to go to. Besides that, nobody wants it."

"Well, I'm gonna do it anyway," I said. "This has gotta be given out somehow." I didn't know how it was gonna happen, but I just believed that we should be payin' attention to these messages from heaven and livin' 'em. I convinced a friend, Vinny, to join me, and we were walkin' around one day prayin' the Rosary when he says, "Why don't we go up to the school? I know the cop that's workin' there, and we'll ask him for a room."

I says, "Nah. I don't want to ask him nothin'." I mighta been converted, but I was still a respectable convict. I wasn't gonna talk to no cops. Well, somehow I end up face-to-face with this cop, askin' him for a room.

"A room for what?" he says.

"So we can have a Rosary group." I felt so un-masculine sayin' that, so I made sure I threw in some attitude. When he asked when we wanted the room, I clenched my teeth lookin' pretty severe: "Every night."

Well, that cop turned out to be a Godsend. He gave us a room whenever it was available, and me and Vinny went in, and we prayed a fifteen-decade Rosary with the meditations according to St. Louis de Montfort. At the end, we said three Hail Mary's in thanksgiving for the room and to praise and glorify the Blessed Trinity in Our Lady's honor. Even on days when we didn't get the room and we was prayin' out in the cold or rain, or whatever the weather, we would say three Hail Mary's and thank her for the room as though we had it.

Within the week, we had seven guys in the room every day, and within a couple weeks, there was twelve to fourteen guys there—every day. Now, these guys weren't afraid of nobody. They could walk anywhere in the prison. They was dangerous, ya know: gangsters, bikers, drug dealers (not the penny ante kind)—knock-around guys, real respectable convicts.

Miracles started happenin' 'cause of our prayer group. We'd pray one mystery of the Rosary, read the daily Mass readings, and I was learnin' this consecration according to St. Louis, so I'd say, "Give it all to Our Lady, and she'll take care of all the intentions of your families, of your heart, and everything." But the guys didn't know about this yet, and no matter how many Hail Mary's and how many decades of the Rosary we said for her intentions, they wanted to pray for their intentions, so this developed into a list for the sick.

More knock-around guys found out we were sayin' the Rosary and would come up and say, "Hey, my kid's sick. Put him on your list, and pray for him, will ya?" One of the guys, a big-time drug dealer from Colombia, had a son born with a hole in his heart, and it couldn't be operated on 'til he was two years old, so this dad asked one of the guys in the prayer group, "Pray for my son, for his operation in six months." As we went along, we said a healing prayer for him, and when the time came for the little guy's operation, they did some pre-operation heart tests on him, and well, he didn't have no more hole in his heart.

We had a pretty tight group. Some of the guys started goin' to Confession. Others were scared, especially to confess things they didn't get caught for because they figured the priest was in with the state. I used to tell them, "No, he's not. I confessed stuff I never got caught for, and he ain't said nothin', and I ain't got no new charges on me." We had serious crimes on our jackets. Some of us had unconfessed murders. Ever seen one of them legal pads? We'd make lists four or five pages long with sins on every line and three- and four-digit numbers in front of them. That's how serious we were about makin' a Confession and goin' forward in life. We started to have First Saturday devotions, and people started goin' to church who hadn't gone in a long time.

We weren't holy men, and prison is not a holy place; but healings kept happenin' when we prayed. Our Lady was showin' us, "You're all a bunch of mess-ups; but see, I love you, because you're trying." That's the way we took it. And when graces came down, we just wanted to do more and more.

In my reading on Medjugorje, I learned how Mary was teachin' the six visionaries about all kinds of things, bringin' 'em along a way of holiness. To me, this was the best form of rehabilitation or habilitation I'd ever heard of. I've been in drug programs, alcohol programs, educational programs, and to me, there isn't anything better than Mary's school 'cause you have to stand before somebody you can't lie to. I found that out when God showed me my choices. You can't lie to someone who knows everything. If I go to some kind of group thing, I can just lie to everybody 'cause my ego is gonna get in the way. So I think goin' to God is the best rehab, and Our Lady was teachin' us in such a tender and loving way. She wanted us to look at God, and she made us want to be loved by her. Somethin' about her way just filled me.

The August before I got outta prison, I was sittin' on my bed, lookin' inside my locker, and noticed a book I hadn't touched, called *The Woman*. It had a picture of Our Lady standin' on the moon, so I opened it up to a part where it talked about this priest in France, in 1830, who was sayin' Mass and was really discouraged because there was only about ten people there. During the consecration, he heard a voice say, "Consecrate this parish to the Immaculate Heart of Mary." He figured it was his imagination, so he shook it off. Well after Mass, he heard it again distinctly, "Consecrate this parish to the Immaculate Heart of Mary." So he announced that he was gonna consecrate the parish, and then a big number, like 400 people, showed up.

I said, "Wow, just imagine if we consecrated the prison. Maybe everybody would start prayin'." So I went to the priest and said, "Father, how about if we consecrate the prison on the Feast of the Assumption comin' up August 15th?" He agreed, and so I wrote one up. I consecrated everybody in that prison: the minimum unit, bayside unit, bayside prison, phase one, phase two—all five prisons, everybody who worked there, everybody who visited there, anyone who brought delivery stuff there, everybody that brought the mail, anybody who drove by, flew over, or came within the vicinity got consecrated on the Feast of Mary's Assumption into heaven.

On the first Friday of November, I came out of one of the minimum units where I was stayin' since I was gettin' out in December, 1990. I'd gotten in the habit of thankin' him every day so I wouldn't rebel against his divine providence. I used to complain about the cold weather comin' up from Florida through Tennessee to New Jersey; but he allows the weather, he allows the mosquito bite, he allows the key to break off in the door so that we can glorify him.

Well, this one beautiful day, I wanted to praise God, so I walked out, looked up, and said, "Bless you, Father, for your perfection. Thank you for the joy you put in my heart." And in the beautiful blue sky, I saw this one cloud veiling the whole prison complex in the shape of a perfect circle, and inside the circle was blue sky and a perfect dove, like someone had airbrushed it. Around the perimeter of the circle were lines extending outward, equally spaced, like a child would draw the sun; but the figure in the middle wasn't being disturbed. I thought, "Wow! Now that really is remarkable." I'm not a fanatic, so I didn't want to get all hyped up 'cause everything is a sign that God exists: the flowers, each other—everything. But I couldn't help but call out to these guys inside who were gonna say the Rosary. "Come on!" I said. "Check this out!"

They walked out, looked up, and said, "That's remarkable." So we prayed the Rosary there, and for those thirty minutes, this dove inside a sun stayed above the prison complex. At the end of the Rosary, as we were sayin' the St. Michael the Archangel prayer, it started breaking up and disappearing.

The next day, I walked to the main prison where we were havin' a First Saturday devotion with the Sacrament of Reconciliation. There was a gang of us now, about twenty-five regulars plus others who were comin' and goin'. Some of these people in the Rosary group were makin' weekly confessions and stuff, and each week you'd catch six-to-ten different guys standin' outside the confessional. While waitin' in line to confess, I started tellin' this one guy what I seen and when I seen it. Three of them looked back at me, and one says, "You were late!" Then they tell me, "A half hour before the dove of the Holy Spirit showed up, there was a perfect heart in the sky right above the prison. Then the heart blossomed out and made the wings of the dove, which looked airbrushed." If I could mistake that as anything other than gratitude from Our Lady, then I'd be blind.

Nowadays, I'm out of prison, and I've been on the outside for many years. Even on this side of those prison walls, it ain't easy tryin' to live a holy life. My memories, my sins, are always with me, and every temptation is right there. To stay safe, I'd have to live in a container someplace. But in his mercy, God has given me a saving grace: a faith-filled wife who has stayed by my side through my greatest joys and my darkest hours. And I know if I cling to the daily love and devotion to Our Lady that I have, and I just concentrate on lookin' at her, I'll do all right.

I still hear from some of the guys from Southern State Prison, and many of them are leading good, Catholic lives in their new freedom. I got word that the prayer group is still thriving at the prison, and Medjugorje is still bearing good fruit there. The inmates sometimes watch a video someone gave them of my testimony at a Medjugorje conference. They pray for me and consider me a brother. Some of the guys in prison will continue to go to church and say the Rosary every day, and some of 'em will fall away. But the thing is we're strugglin'. We're tryin'. Before, there was no tryin'.

While I ain't never takin' lightly the gift God gave me in Tennessee, I come to realize that his greatest miracle is the forgiveness of my sins. That incredible mercy is what keeps me livin' and praisin' him another day. Fr. Hewett once told me that a saint is a sinner who keeps gettin' up. That's what I cling to, the fact that we can always pick up and start again. We can be forgiven—everything. And that's real freedom.

⁓ FOUR ⁓

FATHER PAUL CAPORALI

After Our Lady's Heart

I WAS BLESSED FROM THE BEGINNING with signs of intimacy with Mary. As I awoke to life in a small, industrial town in Italy, called Terni, sixty miles outside of Rome, I noticed that the person closest to me was my paternal grandmother, Assunta, which means "Assumption." She was available twenty-four hours a day to keep an eye on me, while my mother did chores. Every moment of her life, she held the rosary in her hands, even when she was eating. I loved to come down with tonsillitis because I got to skip school and lie tucked in bed. Grandma would sit by my side, telling me inspiring stories about Jesus and Mary, which brought to life the painting of the Madonna and Child by Carlo Dolci that hung above my crib and then my bed.

I had a beautiful mother, too. As the oldest of ten children, she helped care for her siblings, and when she was finally ready to marry and leave the nest, her mother died, so she entered into marriage as the parent of her littlest sister, who was only three years old. Only many years later, when I was seven and my sister was eleven, did she say to me, "I'm your aunt."

"Eek!" Despite that horrifying revelation, which demoted me from big man of the family to little nephew, I loved my "sister," Letizia, very much. We played together often and were quite close. She eventually married and gave birth to a precious baby girl, Rosanna. I also enjoyed my two brothers: Giancarlo, two years younger than I, and Alberto, who came along ten years after me. We were a closely knit family, with my mother taking care of the home, and my father working as an automatic weapons inspector— the consequences of his job never dawning on us. He was often absent from the town, testing machine guns assigned to army border control stations.

To explain the atmosphere of those times, when we went to see the new black and white movies, just a few times a year, Mamma used to advise, "When they kiss, lower your eyes." That was a lovely thing. No media was in the home to distract us or tempt us. No such thing as television existed. The atmosphere in which I grew up was happy, serene, secure, affectionate, disciplined, and loving. The word divorce did not exist in the old country. The family was everything. It was our world.

In Terni, our Catholic religion lived in the streets, not just in churches and homes. Little Marian shrines were scattered on roadsides all over town. Passing them by, I gave the salutation, "Ti saluto madre Maria. Salutami Jesu' da parte mia." ("I greet you, mother Mary. Greet Jesus for me.") a local tradition practiced by most everyone. In May, the month of Mary, the pastor of our parish led an evening Marian procession throughout the whole town. In this festive atmosphere of praise and song, I held my candle among a sea of lights, my heart almost bursting with effusive joy. Also in May, a big, beautiful statue of Mary Help of Christians, with a crown, a scepter, and the baby Jesus in her arms, towered above the main altar of the parish. She was the first Madonna I met, an image which came to St. John Bosco in a prophetic dream and which stirred my affection for my heavenly Mother who always felt so close.

From age seven to nineteen, I was part of the parish boys club, the "Oratorio," which means "place of prayer," run by the Salesian order of priests, founded by St. Don Bosco. To organize the hundreds of boys, the priests grouped us by age and town section, and assigned me to the only group among dozens with a Marian name: The Immaculate Conception. Every Saturday and Sunday, I played games, attended catechism classes, and prayed in the chapel, alongside two or three hundred kids.

When I was fifteen, my father, already an old-timer at stage acting, initiated me into the art by inviting me to join the Oratorio's drama club. I was immediately assigned a small role and did well, so I continued acting in the club's weekly productions held at the parish theater and became one of their top comedians. Being a bit of a rascal, I ad-libbed the lead role in many comedies, sometimes barely reading the script. When dramas were performed, the director encouraged me to come on stage in between acts to tell jokes and funny stories. With no TV and few movies around, the whole parish gathered for the entertainment.

One of my chosen subjects was the imitation of our saintly sacristan, ninety-seven-year-old Ciriaco—a toothless man, almost deaf and almost blind, but enormously devoted to the Church. He couldn't hear himself, so he always spoke his mind aloud. I would imitate his daily, 3 o'clock habit of walking through the Stations of the Cross, making loud comments when he missed some of the stations—"Oops, Lord, where did you go?" Before I stepped on stage, people clapped in anticipation saying, "Paolo! Paolo!" I was happy, thrilled to make them laugh.

At the end of every show, the actors would mix with "the public"—in other words, parishioners, friends, and neighbors. We'd shake hands and welcome a little vainglory, collecting comments and compliments. Two frequent admirers became close to me: my best friend's sister, Mary, who later became a nun, and her friend Lea, who caught my eye. "Oooh, she's nice!" I started thinking to myself.

At age sixteen or seventeen, I asked the director of the Salesian community and the pastor of my church to be my spiritual director. One day, while I was bringing leaflets about a First Friday devotion to families in my neighborhood, he gave me a book of prayers and readings in preparation for First Fridays. In that book, I read accounts of Jesus's mystical life. When I read of his sadness over the rejection he received from the many people he loved, his pain touched my heart so deeply that I began to weep. In that moment, I most likely experienced what Protestant Christians call "the Baptism of the Holy Spirit," or being "born again." Jesus became my very close friend. My apostolic drive to bring others to him increased in fervor, and friends noticed the change in me. I began to serve Mass and found myself in church with my grandmother, more than just on Sundays—times I cherish greatly since she died shortly thereafter. Occasionally, when pausing to stand before a beautiful church statue of the Sacred Heart of Jesus, I would dialogue with him heart to heart. It was abundantly clear. I had fallen fervently in love.

Already a member of the spiritual association of a boys club called the "Catholic Action," I became more fervent in my desire to help Jesus save souls. In Italy at that time, each parish had its own Catholic Action group for women and for men. This national organization encouraged young people to become soldiers for Christ, to work actively and aggressively for the Kingdom of God, for the Gospel, to approach friends and fellow students and invite them to return to Church and to a greater closeness with Christ.

Catholicism was not as fought against then, no other religions being in view. You were a poor Catholic, a rich Catholic, a fervent Catholic, or a negligent Catholic, but you were Catholic. Laxity was pretty common among young people. Using amenities, jokes, and a friendly approach, I wasn't afraid to meet people, especially my fellow students: "Hi Giuseppe, how about going to Mass on Sunday? Oh, come on now, I'll pick you up." Often, I'd ask the greatest or most important question one could ask a fellow human being—a question I still ask today: "Hey, by the way, are you in God's grace?" I invited friends to go to Confession and even tried to lure people away from going into houses of prostitution. The thought of a soul being lost, deeply pained me; I felt Jesus's heart being pierced inside my own.

One day, the director of the drama club, a Salesian priest, came to me and said, "Paolo, read this script."

"Okay," I said. "I'll read it and get back to you." After I did, I said to him, "Um . . . I don't have a role in this! This is all serious."

"I want you to take the lead role."

"You must be kidding. I step on stage and everybody laughs."

"You'll memorize your role this time, and we'll make a go of it."

"It can't be," I thought to myself.

The title of this drama was *Il Grande Silencio* (*The Great Silence*), a three-act play about a saintly priest who spends thirty-two years in prison for another man's crime in order to keep the seal and secret of the Sacrament of Penance. I had to borrow a cassock from one of the Salesian fathers to play the role. I took it home, and after Mamma brushed it, ironed it, and put it on me, she exclaimed with a big smile, "Eee! How beautiful you look as a priest!" I enjoyed her compliment only because I liked to collect admiration and applause; but I didn't have any drive for a vocation to the priesthood, not even a symptom.

I was eighteen when I performed this drama in Lea's parish. Afterward, she echoed with admiration my mother's words to me: "Oh, how good you look as a priest!" I quickly forgot her comment, but I didn't forget her.

Not long after that, my spiritual director asked me, "Paolo, how is your heart?"

Avoiding the depth of the question, I responded, "Okay, Father."

He probed further, "Is there anyone who attracts you?"

"Oh, oh," I answered evasively. "Nobody's there yet."

But his wisdom and recent knowledge prompted him to go a bit further. "Can I name somebody?"

"Oh? Can you do that?"

"Would you like me to?"

Instantly curious, I asked him, "Who could it be?"

"I am not permitted to tell, unless you ask."

And so, with a sudden excitement, I said, "Oh yes, I'm asking, I'm asking."

"Lea Giusti." I was shocked since she had already made a rather deep impact on me.

"Yes, yes," I said and then told him, "Please do not say anything, unless she asks."

He smiled and said, "She already did." Lea, also being a spiritual directee of Father, had obviously asked of him the same favor.

When I left Father's room and dropped into the Salesian community chapel for a little greeting to the Blessed Sacrament, I saw Lea there praying. She turned to me and smiled. I smiled back. So Father not only played the spiritual and emotional director, but also ended up being a matchmaker.

In previous interviews and encounters with Father, he had given me a book to read titled, *A Loro Che Hanno Vent'Anni* (*To Those Who Are Twenty*) by a Hungarian bishop, which I felt proud to read because I was a little over eighteen. One sentence, quoted from an eminent French writer, struck me: "There exists in the world a maiden whom God has destined to you. Do not live in such a way as to bring a heap of ruins in exchange for her flourishing youth!"

That passage had struck me profoundly. I realized that if God knew the number of our hairs, as Jesus said, would he not obviously know who would be the ideal mate for a marriage? When I shared this passage with Father, he commented, "Besides respecting our freedom, the Lord knows what would be best for us. So, Paolo, do not look for your mate in a dancing hall, but in a religious environment." And so, seeking a life partner, I continued to go to daily Mass, and allowing an occasional distraction after Communion, I would look at the people coming back from the altar rail. That's where I discovered Lea's personality, her devotion, her Christian life. I saw her often carrying a rosary in her hand and learned she was a member of a group called "The Daughters of Mary." She was tall and gentle, sweet and very calm, with dark, softly waved hair and thoughtful brown eyes. Keeping an eye on her and engaging her in conversation, I became increasingly interested. Eventually, I fell in love.

One day I met Lea in the lobby of her apartment complex. Being somewhat shy, I began to state a formal, solemn declaration to her, which came out in rather vague terms. With a rapidly beating heart, I said, "I would like to be your friend, your special friend . . . if it does not offend you, I would like . . . one of these days . . . to have our friendship blessed. I mean, eventually an engagement ceremony, or something like that." I looked at her hopefully and could see tears gathering in her eyes.

"Yes," she said, several times. I felt overwhelmed with emotion. In a joyful daze, I accompanied her as she walked to her church to teach preschool. On our way, as we passed by the children's houses, Lea called them out by name to follow her. I grew ecstatic at the sight of this young adult woman, as tall as I, surrounded by a group of little children, with a radiance of innocence comparable to theirs.

A couple days later, I continued my proposal and asked Lea, "Is that really all right? Would you accept me as a possible candidate?"

She beamed, "Yes, Paolo, of course!" I never did get up the courage to say the word "marriage."

Lea surprised me shortly after that as I accompanied her home. We were walking along a street in partial darkness after we had both gone to Confession. Italy had just entered into World War II, and the lights were dimmed for protection against bombing. Suddenly she stopped, looked at me, and said, "Paolo, if you have a vocation to the priesthood, do not let me stand in your way. I would go begging in order to keep you in the seminary."

I answered in mixed humor, "Hey, that's fancy. If you want to get rid of your boyfriend, put him in the seminary."

Looking at me seriously and lovingly, she said, "I mean it. God is first." I never forgot that episode and often wondered what made her come up with that statement soon after I had proposed to her.

In college, I was studying the science of metallurgy, a program sponsored by the huge steel mill factory in Terni. It was 1942. World War II had long begun, and the demands of the war, specifically the increased production of war material, called for the employment of metallurgical engineers. Ours was the first college in Italy that taught metallurgy. The famous Breda Company, which manufactured military products—from armored tanks, to machine guns, airplanes, bombs, projectiles, and all the rest—asked my college for two, newly graduated metallurgical engineers. A friend of mine and myself were selected to move to Milan to work in the Breda steel mill. We accepted the request.

A few days before I had to leave for Milan, Lea and I celebrated our engagement to each other. We were nineteen. Our two families gathered with friends at my house, and Father blessed us in an engagement ceremony. It felt almost like a betrothal, being so formal, religious, solemn, and very joyful—albeit with a little shade of sadness, given I would soon be over 300 miles away. After the ceremony, I hugged my beloved to say goodbye, and I was hoping to kiss her. But, with her instinctive sense of modesty, she gently turned her face and offered me her cheek.

During my stay in Milan, we wrote notes of affection to each other almost daily. Of course, God was intensely present in the beginning, middle, and end of each posted letter. My mom wrote to me, too, though not as often as Lea, and in my correspondence, there was no question about my deep love for both of them. Meanwhile, they grew very close to one another. During the week, Lea often rode her bicycle over to my mom's to see her and chitchat.

In Milan, bombings had already taken place, so a general apprehension hung in the air. I had seen the effect of British bombing in the city: broken buildings and devastated areas. In Terni, every day at 10 o'clock a.m., the alarm sounded, alerting people of this potential call to enter the bomb shelter. My sister, Letizia, and her six-month-old baby girl, Rosanna, numbered among many who had already moved to one of the little towns outside the city to avoid the danger of bombing.

When I returned to Terni for a visit, I wanted to surprise Lea and didn't tell her exactly the date of my arrival. First, I went to see Mom. As I hugged and kissed her, she looked overjoyed and so relieved to see me. Her eyes filled with tears, and I swallowed mine. It felt beautiful to be in her arms. Then I went to see Lea, who lived on the third floor of an apartment building. I knocked on the door of the downstairs entrance, and she called out, "Who's there? Who's there?" But I didn't say anything. She began to descend the staircase as I began to climb. My heart was pounding, and I said to myself, "I'm going to kiss her this time." After all, I was officially her fiancé. When we met, she burst into joyful exclamations, "Oh Paolo! It's Paolo!" and we ran into each other's arms. I made an attempt to kiss her. And in spite of all the joy and excitement, she turned her cheek, smiling, and I kissed her there. I would have to wait. This describes her deep chastity and purity, which at that time was not unusual. Her kisses were saved for marriage.

The next day was filled with indescribable joy. Lea and I spent as much of our time together as we could. We talked about our correspondence and shared our spiritual lives and readings. I described my life up in Milan, and she told me of her days in Terni. She knew that I had gone to Mass every morning to a church near my apartment in Milan, and in a moment of beautiful intimacy, I told her, "The closest I ever get to you is when I receive Communion. At approximately the same time in the morning, when I was receiving Communion in Milan, you were also receiving Communion here. Jesus within you was also within me, and in that moment, I was intensely united to both of you." She beamed, and her eyes filled with joyful tears.

The following day, we went to Mass, and then I accompanied Lea as we rode our bicycles to the supermarket. I remember her looking especially sweet that day, wearing a blue apron-like jumper with a pant skirt, over a yellow shirt with brown polka dots. It was August 11, 1943. The war had imposed ration coupons, and long, slow-moving lines filled the market. I left Lea there, knowing she would have to stay for a long time, and rushed downtown to pick up my graduation picture, having left for Milan before it was issued.

As I was coming back, the alarm sounded—a terrible, terrible sound. In a rush of adrenaline, I hastened home at a furious speed. Bursting through the front door, I yelled, "Ma! Ma! Let's go. Let's go! We need to get into the shelter!" Always with a mother's heart, she thought first of a paralyzed man named Charlie, who lived on the fourth floor, but was spending his days in our first-floor apartment, in case the alarm sounded.

"You go ahead," she said, "and take Charlie with you."

"Ma," I exhorted. "Ma, come on! Let's go. Let's go!"

"I'll close the gas," she answered, "and I'll get the overcoats so that you children don't catch cold in the shelters."

"No! Let's go!"

As I assisted Charlie out the front door, I saw my sister with her little baby, Rosanna, in her arms. Immediately, I asked her, "Letizia, why are you here?"

And she said casually, "Oh, I came down to do some shopping."

I felt so apprehensive inside, but the others didn't. They moved sluggishly, never having experienced a bombing. I said to her quickly, "Let's go. Let's go!"

"I'll wait for Mom."

"No, let's go!"

She remained. So I left with Charlie. We hurried through the gate of the apartment complex; then we crossed the street to a shelter entrance just across from us, hidden under the mezzanine of a large school building. The shelters were well-made tunnels, fourteen yards below the surface, brick-lined, with vertical well escapes connecting to the surface in case blockage occurred. After rounding the side of the U-shaped school to reach the back entrance, I accompanied Charlie into the building and down the first flight of stairs in order to enter the shelter with a crowd of other people. As our feet touched the pavement of the mezzanine lobby, the unthinkable happened.

A whistling roar of bombs and an enormous, prolonged, explosive blast shook the earth violently. That beautiful, sunny, August day became pitch black. Dust and powder prevented any light from entering the long, narrow, mezzanine windows. The long earthquake finally subsided, followed by the crumbling of debris. Then silence—a silence broken only by the diminishing roar of the American bomber's engines leaving behind their deadly cargo.

In the darkness, I began to trace my way back up the stairway. I pushed open the door and held my breath. The darkness was clearing. I could see broken buildings, dust, and nearby, a bomb hole. Close to me, on the left side of the school building, tangent to the path of the school's back door, I noticed a large circular crater. I advanced a little. As I hesitantly stepped toward it, I saw the body of a woman barely emerging from the dirt at the edge of the crater. "Oh, My God!" I exclaimed, wondering who she was, who she had been.

As if walking inside a nightmare, I continued forward along a chain-link fence bordering the school. And then a few yards ahead, by the fence at the entrance gate, I saw many bodies of women, about ten or twelve, piled up along the side of the building. They had obviously been running to find safety in the shelter, but too late. As I stepped closer, I immediately recognized a woman with her tiny baby still clutched under her breast. The back of the baby's head had blown open, and the contents had spilled out onto the ground. It was my sister and her child. In shock, I turned my eyes to look at the corpse next to her. And then I cried out, "Ma questa é Mamma mia!" ("But this one is my mother!") Falling to the ground, I knelt next to her body which lay on its side. As I rolled her over onto her back, her right arm separated from her body. With a trembling hand, I cleaned the brownish dust off her face, and a surge of contempt burst in my heart toward the killers. I wanted to curse the bombers, but a deep urging of Christian pity arose from my emotions, and looking up at the sky I called out, "Father, forgive them. They know not what they do." And I meant it. "They're soldiers," I thought, hanging my head. "They are only doing what they are told." Still kneeling next to my mother's corpse, I raised my eyes again to heaven, to the Virgin Mary. Sensing her spiritually present, I cried out in anguish, "Now, you have to be my mom!"

Slowly, I pulled myself up to a standing position and looked at the other bodies of women, angled and heaped along the way, to see if any were still alive. But none of them were. One body was totally dismembered. I continued to look around. "Lord," I said with desperate hope, "leave me at least Lea." As I heard the distant engines of another bomber's formation approaching, I made my way back into the shelter and began searching for Lea and my two brothers, Giancarlo, age seventeen, and Alberto, age nine. I asked if anyone had seen them, and someone told me that they had seen my brothers. The shelter was in very dim light, and eventually I saw their figures coming toward me down a long, dark underground tunnel. I ran to them, rejoiced, and hugged them close. It was a bitter relief that at least they were still around.

"Did you see Mom?" they asked.

I didn't have the courage to tell them she was dead. I only mumbled, "Let's pray for her."

Another wave of bombing fell on another area of the city farther away, and then silence. After some time, I took my brothers out of the shelter, and with a sunken heart, I brought them over to Mom's corpse. Alberto looked at Mom, knelt, and put his hand forward to clean the rest of the dust from her face. As he felt her cold, stiff body, he asked, looking up at me, "Paolo, where is Mamma?"

I answered, "She is in heaven."

"Are we going to see her soon?" he asked.

"That's up to God," I answered.

As I accompanied them back to the shelter, somebody told me, "Paolo, we saw Lea coming with your mother."

I cried, "Oh no!" and ran back outside by a corpse I'd seen, half-buried at the edge of the bomb hole. Frantically, I began to move the dirt and saw an arm emerge, then part of a bag. Noticing a blue garment on the body, I ripped it to see what was underneath. There I saw yellow fabric with brown polka dots. Sure enough, it was my Lea. "Oh no! Oh no!" I cried out. "Not Lea!" My desolation was too strong for tears.

I continued to unearth her body. She was in a kneeling forward position with one arm around her face and another still holding onto her purse and shopping bag. Her face, protected by her arm, was still clean, pale, with only a little streak of blood that ran from the right edge of her mouth. A sharp sense of despair, loneliness, and searing pain cut into my heart as I stared at her lifeless features. Eventually, wrapping my arms underneath her, I lifted her up and laid her next to my mom's body. Then I rushed to the apartment to gather some sheets so I could cover their bodies.

Standing there sobbing, I instinctively reached for Lea's purse. Knowing that every morning after Mass, she had meditated on the Bible or a spiritual book, I wanted to read the last thing she had read. I pulled out a little booklet I had given her at Christmas, *The Imitation of Christ*, and opened it where she had left the ribbon marker. In a section where the Master speaks to the Disciple, I read, "Do not be overly distressed if I take something of yours; it is mine, I take it back."

"Thanks a lot, Lord!" I blurted out.

Shaking my head, I continued to read further down the page, "And if I take something good from you, it is to give you something better."

I closed the book, threw it into her purse, and cried out, "Lord, what can you possibly give me better than my mom, my sister, her baby, and my Lea? . . . Wrong page!" The Master's words haunted me for some time as I asked myself over and again, "What could the Lord give me better than my loved ones? What could my future be?"

Eventually, after a bombing raid on another side of the city, my dad came by, having run from the factory where he was working. He saw the mess but passed by the corpses without recognizing the people, now wrapped in sheets. When he found me in the shelter, the first thing he said was, "Where's your mom?"

Thinking he had seen her body, I told him abruptly, "She is in heaven."

He put his face in his hands and cried out, "No!"

Realizing he had not seen her, I tried to cover up my words by saying, "I thought you were trying to tell me she was dead. Let's go look for her." Stalling and hesitating, I went back outside with him; and lifting the sheets, he found her. I ran back to the shelter to avoid witnessing him in his throes of pain and despair. Shortly afterwards, in great anguish, he came back down to the shelter to look for his remaining children. We all met, hugged one another, and wept.

With untold sadness, we prepared to bury our loved ones. When Father came to bless the wrapped corpses and saw me standing desolate next to them, he said to me, "You know, Paolo, Lea told me that she had offered her life for the end of the war and for peace in the world." I cried, knowing her piety would have brought her to such an offering of love.

In the panic of the aftermath of the bombing, we decided to leave the city and go to a nearby town, Acquasparta, to stay with the family of my friend who lived with me in Milan. They hosted us for a number of weeks until we found a little apartment there and moved into it. When packing up my things, I noticed a picture of myself looking adoringly at Lea. With a lump in my throat, I turned the picture over and saw she had written something on the back, which I had forgotten: "Caro Paolo, ricordati di me che son la 'Pia' e in caso di morte dimmi un' 'Ave Maria' oppure 'L'Eterno Riposo,'" which translated says, "Dear Paul, remember that I am "Pia" [who in Dante's Divine Comedy asks the poet to remember her after her death], and in case of death, pray a 'Hail Mary' or 'Eternal Rest.'"

With a lump in my throat, I thought, "How strangely and sadly providential." Then I did as she had asked, painfully forming the words, "Hail Mary, full of grace, the Lord is with thee. Blessed art thou . . .," followed by, "Eternal Rest, grant unto her, O Lord, and let perpetual light shine upon her. May she rest in peace. Amen."

I spent most of my mornings in the adjacent town church, attending Mass and receiving the Host with a furious passion, sensing that with Jesus in my heart, I could commune with my mom, Lea, and Letizia. And I wept. Tears and prayer were a great relief for my sorrow, suffering, and loneliness.

After some time, my two brothers, my father, and I began to make visits back to our home city. My father did his best to help us, but we were living a communion of sorrow. Eventually, my mother's youngest sister, Clotilde, a year or two older than Letizia in age, came to live with us, trying her best to play a mother's role. A few weeks later, to help us carry on with our lives, I found a job, locally, watching over the huge storage area of a wholesale furniture factory. Meanwhile, a desire to give myself more fully to God was growing within me. Lea and Mamma's teasing, "Oh, how good you look as a priest!" began to feel like a little hint, and I began to nurture a desire for the priesthood.

"What else could I be?" I wondered. I will never find someone like Lea." Then I said to myself with a little more sense, "This is a great emotional upheaval in your life. Don't make any decisions now." So I left the choice in Mary's hands, telling her, "Mother, do whatever you wish with me. You make the decision, and I'll say yes."

A few weeks later, during one of my quick visits to our broken city, I read the newly exposed posters glued on the walls of Terni by the German occupation troops. The German army, broken, but still holding onto Italy, whose government had already fallen, had issued posters calling for immediate draft all the young men who, for any reason, had been exempt from military duty. These men were to show up immediately to the draft centers, penalty for failure to comply: the firing squad.

Back home, I said to my father, "Ciao, papà. Goodbye."

"Where are you going?"

"Did you see the posters?"

"Oh, it's okay."

"Do you want another grave in the backyard?" I asked him. "They'll find me if I don't go. You know these Germans mean what they say. They are desperate. They are losing the war."

"Don't worry," he answered. "I'm going to hide you."

The next day, we were on our way to the neighboring community of Amelia, a small, medieval town with large, stone, Roman walls surrounding it, and a cathedral perched at the peak of its hill. The town's only entrance—a grand, medieval stone gate, which used to be the drawbridge entrance—still stands, towering over an intimidating ditch, which warded off enemies.

Two Salesian centers existed in Amelia. One, close to the entrance, was made up of a parish, a school, and an Oratorio boys club. The other, on top of the hill by the cathedral, contained an orphanage and a seminary for aspirants to the Salesian priesthood. This house of formation held a grammar school, a high school, and a novitiate, where aspirants spent their first year of preparation for religious profession. It was built on a medieval penitentiary over ancient, underground prisons, whose tunnels provided a perfect hiding place for the seminarians and a number of high officers of the dismembered Italian army.

My father and I arrived at the entrance to the building and greeted the Salesian director, who was well-known to us. Instinct drew me into the seminary chapel, where my eyes rose above the main altar to see a beautiful statue of Mary Help of Christians with her baby Jesus in her arms. Struck by what I knew wasn't coincidence, I knelt, gazing upward, and said in a whisper, "Mamma, tu sei furba e cara. Ecco mi qui. Voglio essere il tuo sacerdote." ("Mom, you are clever and kind. Here I am. I want to be your priest.") I had been brought unknowingly to where I had been dreaming of going.

That day my religious life began. I joined the rhythm of the house of formation and studied in preparation for the priesthood. Sensing Mary's continued protection, companionship, and love, I didn't hesitate to ask favors of her. I was to enter the novitiate on the feast of Don Bosco's birthday, August 16. But I desired to make my religious profession on the celebration of the Blessed Mother's birthday, September 8. I prayed to her to grant me this grace of moving the date—a little extravagant, I knew. A group of novices-to-be were expected any moment from the eastern side of Italy, and providentially, their train schedule was disrupted by the war. When they arrived, a number of days later, the local superiors decided to begin the novitiate on a later date: September 8. "Grazie, Mamma!"

Exactly one year later, again, on that same date, I vowed my life to God in the Salesian Order. On that day of profession, the Father provincial pronounced in his homily that we newly professed Salesians would one day be Marian priests, which felt like honey in my soul.

Being a late vocation at age twenty-four (boys entered into the seminary at a younger age in those days), I was asked to fulfill my three years of "tirocinium," or practical training in priestly formation, as the director of the Oratorio in Terni. Soon I was at home again in the atmosphere in which I grew up. From catechism, to sports, to the drama club, I felt totally absorbed and happy with my apostolic life—my guardian angels being my mom, my sister, and Lea, who were my inspiration and support. By then I could see that God took them to keep them with me intimately, always, wherever I was destined to go.

During this period, I began to think about missionary life. I wanted to share the Gospel with the poor and with those who did not yet know the love of Jesus. My human attachments were all gone, which made the discernment easier for me. With my father living peacefully with his two other children and my Aunt Clotilde, no one would be distraught if I left. My closest ones would come with me.

Being so much a part of the Salesian family since I was a little boy, I'd always known that the Salesians were spreading throughout the world as the third largest religious order in the Church. The largest was the Jesuit order, the second largest, the Franciscans, and less than a hundred years after Don Bosco started the Salesian order, it became the third largest. Due to the war, less men were leaving for the missions, so the Salesian rector major sent exhortations, inviting us to go to the missions in order to replace the vacancies. That convinced me. My desire for missionary work materialized into a formal letter to headquarters, applying for missionary life.

Three years later, when I had almost forgotten about my application, I received a letter of obedience declaring that, in the name of the Lord and by authority of the superiors, I was to go as a missionary to the United States West—to the nation that had been my enemy, to the people who had taken everything from me. I quickly went to the Salesian directory to see where this United States mission was, out of 20,000 Salesian churches in the world. Looking at a map, I narrowed the location down to . . . "Los Angeles! Oh no, Lord! Mamma mia! Los Angeles is Hollywood!" I bewailed. "Mary! Mamma! I wanted to go to the missions to help save my soul, not lose it!"

But obedience is obedience, so I received a ticket for a voyage from Naples for the United States, and I boarded the Luisa Costa, a cargo ship with twenty-one passengers, six Salesian clerics included, who paid for the ship's fuel. Accommodations were rudimental "roomettes," which had been used for soldiers. It took twenty-four days to cross the ocean, and during a rather miserable, wavy trip, everyone got seasick except me and a Rabbi, who slept in the cot above mine. I passed the days walking up and down the deck with the Rabbi in good friendship and helping take care of a little girl on board when her mom felt ill.

After we navigated through the Straits of Gibraltar, our uncomfortable trip became terrifying. The ocean whipped and churned more than the Mediterranean Sea had, and the waves grew increasingly rough and frightening. During the last three days of our trip, a terrible storm tossed the ship violently, and in a critical moment, when the waves rose so high, they looked like they would overtake us, I cried out, "Mamma, if you want me to be your priest, you'd better keep me out of the water!" Eventually, the seas calmed, and we finally viewed with tremendous relief the big lady with the torch in the New York harbor. That day in 1950 was December 8, the feast of the Immaculate Conception.

When I stepped off the boat plank onto American soil, I announced, "Here I am, Mamma. Do what you want with me." I felt that Mary's hand and God's providence had guided me to my new home. I had just left the little three-thousand-person town of Amelia, whose ancient Roman arched gateway reads, Civitas Maria Virginis in Nomine Jesu a Terraemotu Liberata A.D. MDCCIII (City of the Virgin Mary, Freed in the Name of Jesus from the Earthquake of 1703 A.D.). And I was on my way to La Ciudad de Nuestra Señora, la Reina de Los Angeles (The City of Our Lady, Queen of the Angels)—the original title the Franciscan missionaries had given the city so often called simply Los Angeles (The Angels), but mistakenly so. It was Mary's city! From the smallest Marian city in the world, where I began my religious life, I had been transported to the largest Marian city in the world. Coincidence?

A year before I was ordained a priest, I began to ask Mary about the purpose of my past. "Mother," I prayed, "I understand how my having been engaged might be useful for me in helping young people with their relationships and problems; but why did I have to spend four years in college studying metallurgy if I was going to become a priest?" Having worked in Milan at a weapons factory, and having seen firsthand what those weapons could do, I had long since decided that I would never be involved in metallurgy—ever.

A few weeks later, a priest named Father Felix J. Penna came to me and said, "Paul, you are a metallurgical engineer."

I responded, "I was. But I'm not anymore."

"Yes, you are."

"No, I'm not."

"I talked to Cardinal McIntyre and the leaders of industry in Los Angeles, and we have to build a school, and you are going to teach metallurgy."

"No, I am not."

"Yes, you are."

"No, I am not!"

"Yes, you are."

And the vow of obedience slapped me down. Fr. Penna did not take no for an answer, pointing out that I was sent to Los Angeles to help him with this endeavor. "So that is why I'm here," I realized. I had expected to be sent to Africa, Asia, or any other missionary land to work with the poor and to spread the Gospel of Jesus; and now, here I was, next to Hollywood, joining Father Penna at meetings with top industrial leaders. Eventually, the Don Bosco Technical Institute came to be, and there I taught metallurgy for many years.

I hadn't known what to expect when I landed on American soil. In a spiritual sense, Hollywood and its culture felt threatening, and America had a reputation for being a country of world-controlling people. But I found American people to be cordial, benevolent, and generally tolerant— a conglomerate of all kinds and nationalities that could not be generalized. In a moment of intimacy with the Lord, I wrote:

Jesus,

When on that tremendous day, you surrounded me with pain, emptiness and death, I did not rebel. The dear creatures that you took from me were yours. You had given them to me, and I wept and was silenced.

While walking along a different way, you called me, and I answered. I had repeated many times, "Jesus, you are everything to me." And you wanted to prove the truth of my words. And thanks to your grace, you saw that I did not lie.

The words that I first pronounced by the lifeless bodies of the innocent victims were an invocation of forgiveness for the killers. And you wanted to also test those sentiments by sending me to live in their midst. You see, Jesus, that not only did I not consider them forgiven enemies, but brethren; and I love them.

I have kept my promises; you have kept yours.

Thank you, beloved friend, Jesus!

One of Jesus's promises was to carry me into the priesthood by placing me in the gentle arms of his Mother. I was ordained at the age of thirty-one, in the month of Mary, on the thirty-first day—the day Pope Pius II named the "Queenship of Mary" in the year 1954 (now celebrated on August 22). Mamma was making herself obvious. It was also the first

Marian year in the history of the Church, just pronounced by Pope Pius XII, who wanted to commemorate the centenary of the dogma of the Immaculate Conception.

After my ordination in Watsonville, California, I overheard the other newly ordained priests speak of ordination presents from their friends and family in America, so I decided to ask the Blessed Mother in great intimacy, "Mother, I would like to go to Lourdes, France, your holy place, to thank you for all you have done for me up to this point. Would you grant me this present?"

Two weeks after my ordination, I traveled home to Italy, eager to see my family and friends. When I arrived, I noticed posters on the town walls, announcing a diocesan pilgrimage to Lourdes, France—a not uncommon sight, this being the first Marian year. I rejoiced and said to myself, "Yippee-! Mamma heard my request." But, as I read the very large sum on the poster, I mumbled to myself, "A good try, Mom. Thank you, anyway."

With a sweet sense of nostalgia, I celebrated my first Mass at St. Francis of Assisi Church, the parish where I was baptized, received my First Communion, performed plays, and attended Mass, all my life up to the tragedy of the bombing. Half of the townspeople packed themselves into the church, even the communist/socialist mayor of the city, and after the Mass, they flooded the sacristy and filled my hands with envelopes of cash—traditional gifts for newly ordained priests. When I counted the money, I ended up with just a little more than the cost of the pilgrimage. "Thank you!" I whispered, gazing heavenward. Soon I was on my way to Lourdes with a large crowd of my friends, including Lea's father.

Long before my ordination, Lea's mother, Mrs. Giusti, had said to me in earnest, "I would like to attend your first Mass in Italy, and then I would like to die in your arms. I have prayed to my daughter for this." Mrs. Giusti was present at my first Mass in Italy, and then she fell ill. I was expected back in the United States immediately because the Don Bosco Technical Institute was to be started. Passport trouble kept me in Italy for a long time, while Fr. Penna waited, thinking I was prolonging my trip in order to stay longer with family. I still have letters from an irritated Fr. Penna, insisting that I return. After almost nine months had passed, Lea's mom was dying, and I was called to her bedside, where I anointed her, and she expired peacefully in my arms. My sweet Lea had responded to her mother's plea. The very next day, I received my passport, finally stamped by the American consulate, and was on a plane back to Los Angeles.

With my dearest ones always with me and interceding for me, I was able to travel to Italy every four or five years after my ordination, and in each visit, somebody would come by and say, "We're going on a pilgrimage. Oh, Fr. Paul, do you want to join us?" And I was off to give glory to God in Mamma's shrines—Lourdes, Fatima, Loreto, Garabandal, and more. Mary saw to it that I presided at Mass in these holiest of places—a gift that left me euphoric.

In 1977, at age 54, I was asked to be the chaplain of the Blue Army, an association dedicated to following Mary's requests of prayer and penance, when she appeared in Fatima, Portugal. For me, this was another sign of Mary's benevolence toward this humble son of hers.

After I had been a priest almost thirty years, my confidence in Mary had become strong, almost brash. An example of my extravagant trust in her is my first voyage to Medjugorje. It began with one of my trips home to Italy, when I had no sign of a call or chance to visit any of Mary's shrines and only two weeks left of my visit. But after listening to a tape that a friend had given me on the alleged apparitions of the Blessed Virgin in Medjugorje, which had just begun a couple years earlier in 1981, I felt a peaceful desire to go. Knowing that I was gratifying the Blessed Mother, I rushed to the travel agency in Terni and asked for a pass for the ferry across the sea from Italy to Croatia. "What month?" the agent asked.

"Tomorrow," I replied.

He laughed at me and said, "There are no openings for the next few months."

Sensing Mary would get me there, I said, "I have to return to the United States, and I can't wait. Please try to contact the harbor agency where the ferry takes off."

He looked at me with a gently sarcastic smile and said, "No way. You can't go tomorrow." I insisted. Reluctantly, he phoned the office of the travel agency on the other side of Italy in Ancona, and their answer was puzzling, "Oh yes? A cancellation?" He hung up the phone and looked at me flabbergasted. I smiled back nonchalantly.

Then, "Ouch!" I realized I had an American passport and would have to get a visa from the Yugoslavian consulate in Rome, the "eternal" city, where bureaucracy is synonymous with "forever." I called the consulate in Rome, and a man on the end of the line said I'd need to present myself in person. Early the next morning, the son of a dear friend of mine, Edmondo, drove by my apartment, honked, and asked if I wanted to go to Rome with him. "You are a Godsend!" I called out to him. "I'm coming!"

In an hour and a half, we traveled a hundred kilometers and reached the Yugoslavian consulate where lines were long. My friend, conscious of the situation, said, "I'll be back later."

"No. Wait!" I responded. "I'll be only a minute." He smiled at me with pity and stayed.

As I stood in an interminable line of about eighty people, I suddenly saw a consulate employee gesturing toward me to come to him. I boldly went forward to the window, where he asked, "Are you the American I talked to yesterday?"

"Yes!" I yelped, and he stamped and signed my passport. I don't even look American. If that wasn't a miracle, nothing could be.

I went back to my friend's car after only five minutes, and he said, "I told you. It takes longer than . . ." I showed him the stamp in my passport. With a blank look, he started the vehicle.

After a train ride back to Terni, I hopped into a borrowed car and sped to the harbor city of Ancona on the other side of Italy in order to catch a ferry the next day across the Adriatic Sea to the city of Split, Yugoslavia. It was the evening of Ferragosto, the fifteenth of August, a grand Italian holiday celebrating the Assumption of the Blessed Virgin Mary. Every hotel along the Riviera was full. I convinced a woman behind the front desk of a good hotel, to give me a room for the night by threatening humorously to sleep under the couch in the foyer. "You wouldn't want a poor priest lying in your lobby, would you?" With those words, she placed me in a room with peeling plaster and an impaired shower. Elated, I said, "Thank you! It's perfect! I only take a shower once a year in the summer. And in winter, not as often." She laughed.

Relieved, I thought, "Thank God my major traveling difficulties are behind me." But once on the boat, I realized I had only solved two-thirds of my problem. From Split to Medjugorje, I still didn't have any reserved tickets or means of transportation. As I went to the boat's refreshment stand, I happened to sit next to the driver of a Medjugorje pilgrimage bus, which happened to be full, and instinctively, I offered the man a beer. I told him my plight, and he said, "It is not up to me but to the leader of the pilgrimage."

So I looked for the head of the pilgrimage and asked him, "Can you take me with you?"

He answered, "It is up to the bus driver."

I grinned and said, "It's okay with him, if it's okay with you."

The leader, looking half-embarrassed, half-annoyed, answered, "I guess it's okay," and I was on my way.

I spent a glorious week exploring Medjugorje with curiosity and veneration, and I felt Mary's sweet, peaceful presence there like nowhere else I'd been on earth—not even at her other pilgrimage sites. In her palpable embrace, I heard heartfelt confessions, lead prayers, witnessed miracles, and met with the seers. It gave me joy to join Mary's people and to give thanksgiving to the Father who I believe is sending her to be with us in this special way in our lifetime. In fact, I felt so privileged and elated to be in Medjugorje that I returned there three more times.

The events of my life, I have discovered, haven't happened because of coincidence. As long as I have remained in God's grace, Jesus' hand has guided me providentially. All my joys and all my sufferings have been his will. In a diary entry of past years, I wrote:

Jesus,

Nobody surpasses you in generosity and in love . . . You did not ignore my torment because many times you saw me weep in the shade of your Tabernacle. But I never asked you for what you have now granted to me. You know what treasure is the heart of a creature called by the precious name of Mamma! You know it because this creature was close to you for thirty years in an intimacy as profound as it is unknown. And notwithstanding that every throb of your heart and every earthly breath would be for the heavenly Father, you loved her and rejoiced in her. Only your love for the Father was above your love for her. And when you had nothing else to give, you redeemed mankind from up there, from the height of the Cross, with a final effort, you gave your last and most precious treasure, your mother, Mary. "Behold, thy mother."

The greatest thing I ever did was to call out to Mary, at age twenty, when all the women in my life were killed in one instant. As I looked up to heaven and cried, "Now, you have to be my mom," Jesus looked down from his high cross, and suffering with me, he shared with me his Mother. I am a happy priest today, and I owe it to the gift of Mary. I never could have imagined that the words the Lord gave me from my beloved Lea's book would actually come true: "And if I take something good from you, it is to give you something better." But he did. He did.

FIVE

CHRIS WATKINS

Lost Belongings

"YOU'RE A MIRACLE!" exclaimed a religious sister during a retreat I attended in my hometown of Christchurch in New Zealand. She gazed at me with astonishment after listening intently as I raked through the messy beginnings, the unstable childhood, and the self-destructive tendencies of my teens and twenties. Naturally, though, I sidestepped any revelations about my secret self.

Not that I am reluctant to discuss this facet of my personality. It just seemed irrelevant at the time, an unnecessary wandering into that dense thicket of brambles. See, for the best part of fifty years, I have battled with strong feelings of attraction to members of my own sex.

Again and again, throughout my life, I have agonized with the "why?" of this condition. Am I drawn to the male form and masculine presence because of a primarily absent father who, even when he was present, was still distant and never interacted playfully with me? Nowadays, I look with fondness at my three-year-old grandson having a rough and tumble with his father—my second eldest son, and quietly wonder about my own life. If I had enjoyed this same essential element of male-to-male contact in my childhood with my own father, would I have turned out differently, or would I still have been besieged by these ever-present desires and needs?

A baby's gender was unknown until birth in those days when scanners had yet to be invented, but I understand that during my mother's pregnancy her husband was constantly saying he hoped I was a girl. They already had a son, so his picture-perfect ideal was a "one boy one girl" family. Some experts in spiritual healing speculate that the sins and stresses of parents can have a psychological impact upon a baby in the womb; expressed thoughts and desires during pre-birth formation can even affect

99

gender identification. I am left wondering about that, too, with gender confusion playing such a large part in my early years.

                                    ço ও

My very existence began in clandestine circumstances. I was the by-product of an adulterous affair several years after World War II ended. My father was married, so was my mother—and not to each other. To make matters even more complicated, my mother was the wife of my father's best friend. In the indiscretion of it all, I was almost aborted, if my father's story can be believed. There was a period of my early life when I wished this had indeed been my fate. When I was barely two weeks old, my mother handed me over to Dad who was living alone, and he adopted me, legally changing the name on my birth certificate from my mother's surname to his.

Looking back now, I am grateful that I never grew up in my mother's home. She gave me up at two weeks old, and I harbored a fathomless and unacknowledged rage over this for forty years. Additionally, the sight of me would have been a constant reminder to her husband of his wife's infidelity and the betrayal he suffered not only from her but from his closest mate, my father. It could well have been an unbearable childhood.

The reality of bringing up a child by himself soon overwhelmed my father's good intentions. He found it impossible to raise me with live-in housekeepers who came and went, so he, too, gave me up, and I became the Hand-Me-Down Kid. Before I turned ten years old, I had gone through five foster homes. All the stand-in mummies and daddies who offered to care for me soon found that this child who looked the picture of an angel was actually a problem child, a real handful. For no reason ever properly explained to me, I was hurriedly shuffled sideways to new pastures.

In my innocence, while thrown from pillar to post, I was oblivious that my childhood was quite abnormal. From time to time, though, I would wake up sobbing in the middle of the night for no apparent reason. Questioned why I was crying, I couldn't explain.

By the time I was a teenager, I was repeatedly accused of being sullen or moody, but really, I had trouble verbalizing my thoughts and recognizing feelings. I had learned to burrow away inside myself because adults did not like the real me when I let him out. Depression, like a menacing "black dog," as Winston Churchill used to call it, became my deadliest enemy through adolescence, prowling around me with frequent notions of ending it all.

Three bright spots, thankfully, lit up the darkness of those difficult years. The first was an art teacher who discovered my hidden talents and nominated me for an Art Scholarship while giving me private tutoring at his home on the weekends. The second was my greatest form of escapism, acting in the theatre, something I had done since the tender age of eight through to my teens at a high school drama club. The third bright spot, which saved me from abject loneliness, was a special friendship with a very macho boy who lived around the corner from my home.

Yes, Tony was macho, but he continually revealed a softer more affectionate side of his nature as our friendship blossomed. He would often boast, "Chris and I go everywhere together; we are inseparable!" And in time, I grew close not only to him but his large Catholic family as well. His mother took a real liking to me and treated me as her "other son." While Tony was three years my junior, he was somehow older and wiser than my sixteen years, and especially mature in the ways of the world. He was solid, blond-haired, of Swedish descent, and had the looks to go with the personality. I copied his careful sense of dress, his hair style, his pride in his appearance, and he coached me in his methods of picking up girls at discos with sweet-talk and funny lines. I had several girlfriends. But I was play-acting again. It was him whom I adored. I thrived in Tony's company, felt so relaxed and comfortable with him, as we opened our hearts to one another, talking about the most private things, joking and being silly, too. I loved being crammed into the couch next to him, our limbs touching, and the warmth of his presence communicating physically. His mum would often tease us with a kind laugh: "I think you two are in love with each other."

Definitely, by my late teens, I was on a quest for love and security, anxious to get married and settle down. Top priority was a special connection, like I had with Tony, but with a young woman, a soul mate to share the rest of my life. Weddings and happily ever after—that was the social norm in 1968. I'd heard all those wry comments about men in their thirties who were still unmarried and "real Mummy's boys." That definitely was not my future—not that I entirely understood what was suggested there. Such issues were never openly discussed.

When I met Anna around this period of my life, I knew she was the one. By the time I was twenty-two, there were wedding bells; she was only nineteen, a diminutive red-head with a delicious, earthy sense of humor, a creative artistic spirit, coupled with a wisdom and sophistication beyond her years, the product of a convent upbringing. As with Tony, I could explore anything and everything in our conversations. Time froze when we were together. I was truly smitten.

Once it was known that our relationship was serious and our engagement became official, I was readily absorbed into Anna's large Catholic family circle with great warmth. Wedded bliss, however, went out the window within months for me. Marriage opened a can of writhing worms, with unimagined difficulties surfacing on every front. I had no idea how to cultivate the emotional intimacy necessary for a happy union with a spouse. I had everything I had ever dreamt of, and now something inside me was pushing it all away. I was suffocating: feeling lost at sea in suburbia, overwhelmed by the expectations and pressures in this new role I had taken on, hemmed in by in-laws on all sides. That's when I started sinking, the black dog locking its teeth into me and dragging me under again.

My twenties became a decade of turmoil. Within the first year of our marriage, my new wife began attending a Bible study and prayer group, and then she returned to regular Mass. I reacted badly. Her sudden churchgoing offended my "free thinking." I had thought she was unbound by convention, like I was, not a "victim of the narrow, oppressive, simplistic views" of a belief system that I had gladly abandoned at age thirteen. Yes, I had agreed to get married in the Catholic Church to please Anna and especially her mother, whom I really respected, but I remember sitting through the marriage instruction course, thinking it was one big intellectual yawn. I couldn't believe that people still subscribed to such antiquated ideas and superstitions—the endless thee's and thou's and thou shalt not's of Christianity were a hangover from the medieval era, no longer relevant to everyday life in the swinging 1970s! And when I learned that Catholics believe the consecrated bread and wine to be the REAL Body and Blood of Christ, I was both shocked and amused: these people practice cannibalism, I blinked.

Anna's decision to take her faith more seriously became my own personal challenge. Christianity was just a little too simple and obvious. I was determined to undermine her efforts. I was a truth-seeker, but I wanted to find my own answers. Before long I was visiting psychics and embroiled in all manner of occult research, Eastern mysticism, reincarnation, UFO culture, everything we now call New Age teachings.

The aftermath of my spiritual dabbling was a depression of such unimaginable depths that I believed I would never recover. There was only one way I could see to end this abyss of gloom. As if in a trance, I walked to the nearest pharmacy one morning, bought a large capsule of sleeping tablets, went home and quickly downed all of them.

Anna had an inexplicable, but urgent, compulsion that morning to desert her workplace and drive home. After finding me unconscious, she leapt a six-foot fence—unexplainable again—to use a neighbor's phone. In the hospital, my stomach was pumped, and I found myself back in the grey vacuum of nothingness I had been trying to escape from, with the further discomfort of a psychiatrist probing me: "You have only been married a short time, you should be radiantly happy. Why aren't you?" With surly, youthful arrogance, I muttered, "I dunno. You tell me. That's your job isn't it?" The nursing staff had no time for me, treating me like rubbish. If he wants to die, then let him die, was their attitude, adding to my burden of worthlessness. I was discharged from the hospital with a prescription of antidepressants, which made me feel even more alienated and disconnected. This was compounded by regular rounds of electric shock treatments, leaving me dazed and confused.

Was it any wonder that several months later, I gulped down mouthfuls of the prescribed medication with as many sleeping tablets as I could physically stomach? This induced a massive stroke. Fortunately for me, I was in the hospital when the stroke occurred, and doctors were able to act immediately. I almost died, was considered beyond help, the slim chance of recovery meaning permanent damage. Vaguely, I recall searing white clinical lights and my stumbling about on a walking frame to get my legs functioning again. Little did I know that my wife's family and friends were down at the local church praying the Rosary in great earnest.

Having miraculously survived two serious suicide bids, I emerged from all this with a strong realization that something—or possibly Somebody?—valued my existence. Perhaps there was a God, after all, who cared about me, and who had saved me. My best friend at the time said, "You've fallen as far as you can go. When you hit the bottom, there's only one way to go, that's up!" Those words comforted me. With renewed determination, I tossed all my remaining antidepressant tablets down the toilet, picked up the pieces, and got on with life.

I was turning a new corner in my journey toward the light, but rather than a steady climb, it became a rollercoaster ride. From the illusory heights of my junk food spirituality and its grim consequences, I sidetracked into hedonistic excesses. Everything became a blur of drunkenness, partying, and finally drugs and adultery. My recovery from suicidal thinking was signaled by a switch in career, from retail advertising to the world of commercial radio. In my new work place, I loved rubbing shoulders with television and broadcasting personalities. I attained a degree of celebrity myself in terms of creativity, winning awards for my commercial writing and production, and thereafter being pursued by other radio networks. From a fairly sincere, introspective, and idealistic twenty-five-year-old, I degenerated into this abominable, egocentric guy, hell-bent upon social indulgence and physical gratification.

At a private bar reserved for our Friday night let-your-hair-down antics, I drank myself senseless one night and got entangled with a sports announcer who had a reputation for "liking the boys." Although I allowed him to seduce me later at his home, not much really happened, except that this incident unlatched the basement door to my long-denied homosexual inclinations. This tentative encounter gave me a rush of adrenalin, an incredible euphoric sense of release and freedom, as if my true self had awakened at last. This initial homosexual contact led to two further relationships, which became unhealthy attachments. The chemistry was so electric that every living moment of the day was torn apart by an ache to see each of the men involved, to the point where I was virtually stalking the two of them. It became a craving that consumed me and brought utter misery.

Fortunately, I was saved from my obsessions. My path crossed with a young man from a Catholic background, once again, and a firm bond of true friendship developed. I had noticed this gravitation of mine toward Catholic people—they seemed to have some indefinable "X" factor. Patrick brought with him a real respect for what was left of my integrity. His attentiveness and belief in me somehow curbed any further downward slide on the muddy slope of infidelity with other men. As a radio DJ, he had a wonderful ability to connect with people, and he is the only heterosexual man I've ever known who could clasp my hand and tell me he loved me. He was warm, intelligent with aesthetic tastes that paralleled my own—a man after my own heart with a tremendous sense of humor.

We became a creative team: I wrote the movie spoofs and the mock soap-opera serial scripts, and Patrick could skillfully bring them to life with great comic timing, impersonating everyone from Jimmy Durante to Snagglepuss. Although we did, stupidly, venture into an LSD trip together one weekend, his was a strong and healthy form of mateship. I began to shake off the magnetic pull to the then-illegal homosexual underworld to which I had been introduced, and to reform my behavior.

Meanwhile, my much-neglected wife at home with our two baby boys, announced that a third child was on the way. This coincided with my successful application for a transfer within the radio network to our northernmost city of Auckland. Anna, very reluctantly, agreed to uproot everything and join me.

Within months, our family had expanded with another child, a beautiful daughter whose birth brought tears to my eyes. I made an inner vow never to get caught up in the same social web of irresponsibility that had ruined things in Christchurch. No drinking! No lingering outside strict working hours! No time-consuming friendships outside my marriage!

My firm stand of reform endured for a season or two, and then gradually, without realizing it, my boundaries began to blur again. New friends in Auckland were drawing me, not against my will, I must add, back into smoking marijuana during my lunch break, and ultimately to a weekend away at a music festival, which brought disaster. During a police raid, I was arrested for drug possession. After a warning from my boss, I resigned, and in angry defiance, joined the rival "pirate" radio station, where drug-taking was a way of life.

This period was typified by a return to my contemptuous dismissal of anything Christian. In our home, Anna had hung lovely Byzantine-style icons of the Sacred Heart of Jesus and the Immaculate Heart of Mary, and I hated them. I ripped them from their antique frames and used the pictures as backing for surrealistic Dali prints. There was only one thing I hated more: Anna said she put God first in her life, and I insisted that surely I should be her number one!

By the summer of '79, I had graduated back to "acid," a brand of LSD, called California Sunshine. Strangely enough, I emerged from a "trip," the last one I would ever take, with my mind open to the first glimmering of faith. Something began to dawn on me: if God was truly God who had created the entire universe, then surely, I reasoned, he would have no trouble entering into his own creation, taking on human reality and becoming one of us. I remember delving into the Twenty-third Psalm, and it spoke personally to me—the first instance of Scripture ever taking on any relevance. But the after-effects of LSD also had me bordering on madness, scrambling to reassemble the scattered shards of my psyche. My home life was playing second fiddle, once more. At work, I was under relentless pressure for creativity, and on the home front, under pressure as well. Our fourth child was on the way, which caused panic and desperation for me. I pushed and persuaded Anna to have an abortion, totally unaware of the gravity of such a decision. Anna's Catholic convictions and natural obstinacy combined to help her withstand my bullying tactics.

Something had to give. This was to be the turning point. One night, I returned home after a long day of writing and producing in the recording studio, followed by an evening of unwinding, getting high on marijuana and alcohol. Under the influence of this lethal mix, I tried to convince Anna that God was a seven-headed dragon, just like the emblem I bore on my wallet. When she vehemently resisted my bizarre notions, I interpreted this as rejection. I wanted to shake her out of her narrow-minded complacency and open her to the infinite possibilities of my cosmically enlightened supremacy. So maddened, so frustrated was I by her refusal to "believe in me" that my protest escalated in ferocity, and before I knew what I was doing, I was physically shaking her, pushing her against the kitchen wall, my hands around her throat.

There was rage deep inside of me, quite unknown to me—thirty years of stored-up fury at my mother's rejection, and all of it was transferred in that maelstrom moment upon Anna. At the height of the outburst, I experienced what psychologists call "disassociation": I saw myself briefly from outside of myself, like an overview, and was shocked to the core that I was in the throes of assaulting the one person I loved the most.

Anna was traumatized, terrified. I could only focus on my own inner turmoil, as I recoiled in horror from what I had done. Collapsing on the couch in the lounge, overcome with disbelief, I sobbed inconsolably, hot tears of remorse. I never thought I was capable of such actions, having always seen myself as a peaceable, nonviolent person. What was happening to me?

That was when I knew beyond a doubt that I needed help—real help! Any remaining shred of self-reliance had run aground. I mean, how many times had I promised to reform myself and failed miserably? Who to turn to? Not psychologists. My problems were of spiritual origins, I was convinced. Something told me that an intense battle was going on for my soul. And I recognized that it would take more than human resources to rectify matters. One thing was for certain: I would never touch drugs again—never, ever.

Later that night, the lid came off my secrets. I admitted to Anna all my indiscretions. She was shocked. I was ashamed. The next day when I returned home from work, the house was empty. A goodbye note from Anna said she was leaving me. I was shattered. After visiting her and the children in a Women's Refuge Camp, I learnt that they were flying back to Christchurch to Anna's family. I was on my own. My world was caving in. "I am thirty years old and so screwed up," I mumbled, "an absolute mess!" Somehow, I thought, I must hand my life over to God. Into my mind came the picture of a sweet old Croatian priest, Fr. George Marinovich, who had visited us when we first arrived in the neighborhood, two or three years before. Despite my strong anti-Christian feelings, I had warmed to him when he'd prayed a special blessing on Anna and me. I knew where he lived, only two blocks away in the parish presbytery, so I decided to look him up. Here I was, turning for help from what I had once cynically called, "the grey institution."

Enter Mary, the Blessed Mother. On Saturday, December 8, the feast of her Immaculate Conception (as I would come to note several years later), Fr. George arranged for me to meet a man who had a reputation as a "charismatic healer." On that day, I biked for ten kilometers through hilly suburbs to Auckland's Franciscan friary to seek out a monk named Brother Raymond.

I was expecting to meet a Padre Pio type of character in brown habit with supernatural powers, but instead I shook the hand of an ordinary, unassuming chap in a mountain shirt and overalls—very disappointing. Perhaps I'd been given the gardener by mistake? We settled down side by side on a park bench in the picturesque friary grounds, and I spilled out my tangled life story to him. He was about fifty, I guessed, and had a gentle non-invasive manner. On his lap was a well-weathered Bible, and he drew my attention to a few passages, mostly about "believing" as the key to salvation.

At the heart of all my problems, Brother Raymond told me, was the chronic pain of my mother's abandonment. This rejection was a wound that needed the healing touch of the Risen Lord, and it took no persuasion on his part for me to agree to the solution. He and a fellow "charismatic" would pray over me and invite the Spirit of Christ to enter into my past, starting from the womb right through to the present day. All I wanted to know was, when? And how soon? There seemed an urgency, as if the devil himself was at my heels stirring up apprehension and fear.

I only had to wait four days. It was December 12, the Feast of Our Lady of Guadalupe, and on this second occasion, Brother Raymond was decked out in full regalia, his brown Franciscan robe falling ankle-length to his sandaled feet, wooden rosary beads swinging at his side, Holy Bible in hand. The sight scared the living hell out of me. When he and his friend locked the door of the room as they entered, I wanted to flee, untold fear clutching my insides. They both gave me the option of leaving, but I was torn between these strong anti-feelings and the equally strong desire to be healed, which won out. For hours, it seemed, these two men prayed over me, concentrating especially on painful and crucial moments from my past, as I was cleansed by a continual stream of my own tears. During this whole process, the very air in the room seemed electrically charged with another unseen presence. I had no doubt whatsoever that Jesus Christ existed, was resurrected from the dead, and was tangibly there with us!

When I finally curled up in a bed in one of the guest rooms at the friary, weak and exhausted, emotionally spent, I was conscious that something inside me had changed. Several years further on, I learnt the significance of this special date, December 12—how Mary's appearance in the New World of the Americas in 1531 inspired eight million pagan natives to flock to baptism in the name of Jesus Christ and convert from a serpent-god who demanded infant sacrifice—and the parallel was not lost on me!

I slept a heaven sent sleep that night, and the following day, when I returned to work, the receptionist, an ex-nun who knew nothing of what I had experienced, said to me, "You look like a great burden has been lifted off your shoulders!"

It took another three years before I fully and resolutely converted to the faith. Not long after that monumental night of healing, on the advice of Fr. George, I moved out of the lonely family home until I could get myself in order. Perhaps felicitously, I rented an apartment in St. Mary's Bay, and nearby, there was a steep, almost vertical stairway called "Jacob's Ladder," which descended into the central city. I liked all the symbolism.

For nine months, Anna and I were apart, and during that time, my youngest son was born. I began attending Mass each morning at a chapel in St. Mary's Bay until the priest was advised that I was unlawfully receiving Holy Communion. Irate and rebellious, I thought, "So the Catholic Church doesn't want me. All right! I don't want it!" The Holy Bible and all my Christian books by the bedside became buried under such volumes as *God is Gay*, which infuriated my wife's Catholic sensibilities.

Two steps forward, one step back, on my winding track out of the woods toward the narrow path of faith: I gave full expression to my "natural" inclinations and "came out," living the homosexual lifestyle. Making up for lost time, I allowed myself to be used and abused. I had to learn, as always, by burning my fingers. Eventually, I came to my senses, like the prodigal son, disillusioned with the whole supposedly "gay" subculture and its superficiality, mindless promiscuity, back-biting bitchiness, and dalliances. I was looking for true love, and it wasn't to be found there. All at once, I longed to return to normality, to reclaim the married life I had abandoned and the children I had been missing. I was haunted by a promise I had made to myself, around the age of twelve or thirteen, that if I ever had children of my own that they would have a mother and father and both under the same roof!

Anna gave me sanctuary. As much as she was hesitant about our reunion, she also recognized my need at the time. Only weeks after our marriage resumed, I was provided with a steady job, which led back to radio advertising. In the year that followed, our home was visited by a pilgrim Virgin of Fatima, and I sneaked out of bed in the middle of the night, knelt beneath Mary's statue, and begged for financial assistance for our growing family. The very next day, incredibly, I was given a substantial raise, along with back-pay dated back several months. I was dumbfounded.

A definite milestone on my journey back to God was the day I met English pop-star, Cliff Richard. I had always been a great admirer of him, and attending his press conference in 1982, sitting right beside him, I was in awe as he revealed what the Christian faith meant to him. "I wish I could believe as implicitly as he does and be so confident in witnessing to such faith," I yearned.

Within six months, this prayer of my heart began to be answered. At the Catholic school where my children were pupils, there was a fascinating film evening which featured the alleged apparitions of the Virgin Mary at a tiny hamlet called Garabandal in Spain. Unlike Lourdes and Fatima, these particular mystical events had occurred between 1961 and 1965, in my own lifetime, and actual film footage added to the evidence. I was gripped by the whole story, even buying a book on the subject, called O *Children, Listen to Me.*

Everything I was to read in that book had a huge impact on me. On the front cover were the reported words of the Virgin Mary: "What God loves above all is humility. What displeases him above all is pride." Those words touched a raw nerve. I felt convicted. I knew I was guilty of pride. Little did I know that I was soon to be humbled; my change of stance, now admitting that the Catholic Church may be right, was a step in that direction, and wasn't that humiliating enough? Worse still, my deadliest secret: I was reading Catholic literature, and—heaven forbid!—poring over the Bible in stolen moments. Wasn't this the same man who had once taunted his wife when he found her constantly studying her Bible at bedtime, "Fair go! You're not reading that damn book again are you? It's time you broadened your mind a little!"

The one thing that truly affected me about Garabandal was the way the Blessed Virgin purportedly reinforced all the basic teachings of the Catholic Church by practical demonstrations to the four young visionaries. Apart from the fundamental virtues, like modesty and purity, she upheld the essential beliefs in original sin, heaven, hell, purgatory, and the sacraments, giving extra-special emphasis to the Holy Eucharist.

All these teachings began to make more and more sense to my skeptical mind. I was receiving graces, unbeknown to me. I was intrigued to learn that the Catholic Church did not originate with the Emperor Constantine, as mistakenly held by some Christians who think he was the first Pope. Instead, the Church could be traced right back through an unbroken line of popes to the apostle Peter himself. Even the Encyclopedia Britannica conceded this fact by listing every name in the papal succession. Furthermore, I began to realize there was a consistent message from the Virgin Mary, "Pray the Rosary." The places where she appeared already maintained a great devotion to this age-old prayer—always Catholic places, I noted.

A few days after my thirty-third birthday in 1982, I approached Fr. George about becoming a Catholic. It was all very undercover, a real embarrassment. Anna told me, years later, that this move of mine coincided with her ultimatum to God, "If you don't do something about Chris, I'm leaving him. I give up on him. He's all yours. Only you can save him!" She was flabbergasted when I told her the next day that I was about to receive instruction to become a Catholic. Nevertheless, she was reserving her judgment. Over the last few years, she had heard a good number of broken promises from my lips.

My prayer life grew daily. I became the teary-eyed recipient of many answered requests. The Holy Spirit took me on a guided tour of everything Catholic, revealing so many truths through Scripture and through the concerted efforts of Fr. George and Brother Raymond at the friary.

Both these men had a special love for "Our Dear Mother," as Fr. George called her. Knowing the maternal absence in my life, he wasted no time in quickening my spirit to a consciousness of her. "She's Mum," he once chuckled, hugging a life-size statue of her. Before long, I was consecrated to the Immaculate Heart of Mary and wearing the Brown Scapular. Early one morning in August, I clumsily attempted to pray the Blessed Virgin's Holy Rosary and, after I finished, was astounded to find on Anna's Church calendar that it was the feast day of St. Dominic to whom Mary had appeared and given the Rosary in the thirteenth century. This soon became a daily habit of mine, the prayerful circuit of the rosary beads. Since then, many milestones in my onward pilgrimage have occurred on Marian feasts and anniversaries—just to remind me, I'm sure, that my Mother cares.

So many little miracles began to enter my day-to-day walk in the Spirit: prayers answered, internal visions, confirmations. It was a wondrous time. My life, my attitudes, my understanding of everything was radically shifting; my perception of reality metamorphosed and broadened, my values turned upside down and inside out. So many truths were dawning on me, so many long-held misconceptions about Christianity disappearing, my old cherished notions overthrown. My love for the God who saved me was unbounded. Every Sunday when I knelt at Mass, what an emotional time it was, with deep surges of repentance sweeping over me. Frequently, I would feel "touched"—anointed by the Holy Spirit, and tears would roll down my cheeks, especially when the priest consecrated the Host. At that time, I had no conscious idea that Christ truly became present in Holy Communion, even though I had joked about cannibalism all those years earlier. When I was later instructed on the divine nature of the Eucharist, it came as no surprise, confirmed, as it was, by those spiritual glows at consecration.

On Friday, October 15, that year, I was formally received into the Church. There was no need for baptism. I was christened as a baby in the Anglican faith of my parents and the Anglican baptism is valid in the Catholic Church. A few days before Christmas, in a private ceremony with the Bishop of Auckland, I took "Francis John" as my confirmation name. The occasion was quite unannounced. I had been helping assemble the crib scene before the altar, repainting a host of angels and the Bethlehem backdrop, when I had glanced up at the Tabernacle and saw this momentary image of a white dove hovering there. Seconds later the church door opened and Fr. George's housekeeper appeared. "Run home and get changed, Chris," she said, "the Bishop is coming to confirm you!" It was the most perfect, deeply meaningful Christmas I had ever celebrated. I had this overwhelming sense of belonging. I had truly "come home."

For several years afterward, I enjoyed a tremendous "honeymoon" period with the Heavenly Bridegroom. Anna grew more trustful that my faith had genuine roots and was not just another passing phase. I was taking my home life with the children far more seriously, and we were attending Mass as a family each Sunday. For me, it was daily Mass according to Fr. George's prescription for eradicating thirty years of contamination: "Your principal weakness and greatest foe is sensuality," he said, "so you need the daily healing touch of the Divine Physician." During my initial conversion to Catholicism, I had resigned from radio and started work at a home for sixty disabled people, recently opened in our suburb, only walking distance from my front door. This lasted for four years, until Anna was suddenly hit by a debilitating illness, which left her weak and confined to bed for six months, and we resolved to sell our house and return to the wider support of family in Christchurch.

It was while my father, in his late seventies, came to live with us after our shift back south that several things culminated. I was keen to cultivate greater family dynamics, encouraging Dad as a grandfather and trying to close the gap between him and me, but it was intensely difficult. I had arranged for a special Mass to be prayed for the healing of the family tree, and this happened, as it turned out, on my mother's birthday. Quietly then, I did some detective work and located her whereabouts. I met her for a lunchtime coffee, and we exchanged many words. It was so good to finally put a face to the mother I had never known, to scotch all those stupid fantasies that she was perhaps a famous actress or suchlike. I recognized some of my own characteristics in her and experienced a real sense of identity, that I was more like her than my father. As we parted, I gave her a sketch I had made of Jesus and his Sacred Heart that she tucked in her handbag, and smiling, she said, "I love him too!" Then she said: "This is the only meeting we will ever have. My husband is forbidding me to see you again."

To hear this crushed me with disappointment, but I said nothing. I was saddened that she would never meet or know her four grandchildren. "Her loss," said Anna later that evening. No sooner had I told her what my mother had said that I felt an incoming tide of depression, wave after wave, washing over me. The old black dog was back on the horizon, circling once more, closing in on me.

Other unwanted feelings were resurfacing, too. My belief that God's grace had healed me from same-sex attraction was proving to be an illusion. Such allurements and thoughts had simply been pushed underground in favor of the more pressing needs of providing for and raising a family. While every spare moment was keenly spent in pro-life interests and fostering devotion to the Rosary with a Fatima statue, which I circulated in our parish, I found myself distracted by second looks at handsome faces and disturbed by the sight of more and more exposure of male flesh in the media. I went to Confession to repent about these upsetting temptations without being specific. My ambiguous remarks could easily have been referring to women not men. "Maybe I just have a heightened appreciation for the beauty of God's handiwork," I suggested to the priest who chuckled. "Oh dear, you wouldn't be laughing if you knew the full truth," I thought. For seven or eight years since Anna and I had reconciled, I had kept everything firmly in place.

I reached burn-out point in 1990. After a knee-cartilage injury and operation, I had opted for working temp jobs piecemeal, often from sunrise to midnight, dovetailing nurse-aide shifts with freelance writing for television and for a friend who owned an advertising agency. Understandably, with budgeting for a family of six, Anna was unhappy with the unreliability of an income that was far from a regular wage. All these issues eating at me, I retreated to the Redemptorist Monastery for a week's break from everything, taking with me a young, homeless street kid, whom I had been supporting in his efforts to quit glue-sniffing. Unknown to me, Anna suspected I was back into old habits and was having a relationship with him. Nothing could have been further from the truth. I had met him one morning at the Cathedral when we were praying the

Rosary for those "on the margins of our society," and helping him seemed part of my Christian outreach.

When I left home with a few clothes and some devotional material for the retreat, I had this overwhelming feeling in my spirit—a feeling I was trying to dismiss—that I was never going to return to the family homestead. Anna phoned me three days later at the monastery and told me she did not want me to return. She wanted a legal separation, a clean cut, no post-mortems. It was over. Eighteen years of marriage—gone! I was reeling at the prospect of legal separation, absolutely gutted. I sobbed and cried for two days in the chapel, and then my grief turned to anger. I had done everything in my power to make up for the first eight years as the miscreant—and this was the outcome for all my efforts! Today, I can understand Anna's frustrations with me. She needed a solid steady sort of guy who brought home a dependable weekly pay packet, who did not suffer from all the inner tensions that frequently immobilized me. In truth, I was the fifth child in our family, a forty-something man-boy.

My devastation was immeasurable. I had built my whole sense of belonging around Anna and my children. Overnight, my homemade insurance against a legacy of insecurities had been pulled from beneath my feet. It took marriage collapse, however, to force me to face the truth about myself, to confront with honesty my own limitations, my inability to cope with stress, my issues of abandonment by both parents, and of paramount importance, recognition and self-acceptance of my re-closeted sexual orientation.

Several months down the line came the most terror-stricken moment of my forty-two years. At a family gathering organized by a family-court counselor, he encouraged me to disclose my darkest secret to all four children. "How do you feel about Dad now?" he asked, after my stark confession. My second eldest son, fifteen years-old at the time, sprang to my support and moved me to the brink of tears. Nathan didn't hesitate. In a very matter-of-fact tone of acceptance, he said, "He's still Dad."

Anna's spurning, which duplicated my mother's rejection, opened me up to the feelings I had been denying and sublimating for ten years. The hurt, the bitterness and anger—I had so much anger—gave rise to a rebelliousness that laid bare a pet notion of mine, which had never been fully addressed, that a male soul mate would consummate my heart's longing. At a city bus shelter one evening, such a person appeared to have crossed my path. His name was Matthew. We fell into talking, and when he caught the same bus as me and then alighted at the same bus stop, I was amused by this coincidence.

Significantly, one of our first conversations was about the "so-called fairer sex." Like me, Matthew was recovering from a break-up with a woman he had been living with, so together we seethed about how Western females had become so aggressive and so domineering, poor imitations of men. But Matthew was not spiteful by nature. Sweet and sensitive, he had a generous spirit and a heart of gold. I would share the next ten tumultuous years of my life with him.

My world totally crumbled during the first year of our relationship. As I "came out of the closet" and gradually admitted to friends and family the new direction my life had taken—that Matthew and I were a male couple living together—I swung between gay pride and self-effacement, soaring emotions and despondency over my losses. A Christian counselor, who prayed with me during that time, commented that I was like someone who'd lost a great treasure. He was right. I was stretched on a torture rack between heaven and hell. Seeking to make spirituality and sensuality compatible bedfellows, I wanted "life in the Spirit" with God, and I wanted Matthew as well, because I felt so loved. My arguments went like this: "My lifelong desires are being fulfilled. Why should God want to come between me and this man? We're made for each other!"

But the eternal tussle continued. I had to explain away those convicting passages of Scripture. "The Old Testament references to fornication and the abomination of man-to-man sex are about promiscuity," I'd protest, "not about loving gay unions as we know them in modern times." To justify my lifestyle, I even began writing a whole book called, *A Damned Fine Loving!* "If you read the story of Sodom and Gomorrah," I wrote, "you'll see it's about violent and inhuman gang rape. The men of Sodom were depraved and animalistic, their behavior an offense against love. And as for St. Paul's remarks in Romans 1:27, let's be honest, he's homophobic, probably homosexual himself. . ." And so it went on. For a short spell, my conscience would be quieted, and then it would start up again.

Despite my own spiritual struggle, Matthew was attracted to Catholicism. He was fascinated by the richness of its culture and had great admiration for Pope John Paul II (now St. John Paul the Great). Right from the start, though, I vowed I would never foist my beliefs on him, that I'd only speak about the faith if he asked questions. Which he did. Many times.

115

Sadly, Matthew suffered from reoccurring psychotic episodes, and eventually I began to pray that God would somehow extricate me from my complex entanglement with him. On December 8 (the feast of the Immaculate Conception), I came across a leaflet in a Catholic bookshop, concerning Devotions to Jesus King of All Nations. The promise of "powerful and unprecedented effects" was attached to a novena of Holy Communions in honor of Jesus, under that title. The very next day, when I went to Mass and began to pray the novena, I was inundated with more doubts about my lifestyle. On the last day of the novena, I was in for the surprise of my life. Upon coming home after receiving Holy Communion, Matthew told me he had something serious to discuss with me. "I want to become a Catholic," he said. "I want to go for instruction and be baptized." I nearly fell over backwards, especially at the next piece of news: "I also want to receive Holy Communion, and that's the tricky bit. I'm sorry, Chris, but we'll have to end our sex life. I couldn't possibly go to Communion and be sexually active. It had to come to this eventually, anyway. So how do you feel about celibacy?"

I remembered all the times I had been to Communion while sexually sinning, and I could only admire Matthew's stand. "He's got more integrity than I," I thought ruefully. Three days later, I went to a full and proper Confession. Heart in mouth, I wandered over to the rectory, but thankfully, the priest didn't sound judgmental when I spoke about my homosexuality. Instead he acknowledged mildly, "So you've sinned with another man."

Matthew was received into the Church not long after we split up, and for four years I practiced celibacy, attending a weekly group called Courage, a worldwide, spiritual support network for those who experience same-sex attraction but wish to live chaste lives in accordance with the Church's teaching.

For the first time in my adult life, I was a single man and living alone, not needing to make compromises, not answerable to anyone but God's Spirit and his directions. And then this hankering in me arose, a nagging daydream of sharing my life with someone again. Maybe it was because I knew the last vestiges of youthful vigor were on the wane. Maybe I was egged on by people around me who said I deserved to have someone to love. I had applied for an annulment, which the Church duly granted, freeing Anna to remarry, if she wanted. This she did. But for myself, I was too honest to pretend I could entertain such thoughts ever again. Although

116

women seemed to be attracted to me, I could not possibly put another woman through the same hoops and heartache, as I had with Anna.

Through my network of friends and my work as a community caregiver, I met James, a fellow believer, although not Catholic, a very special, sensitive man. It took eighteen months of regularly seeing each other before we moved into a townhouse together. I became heavy-hearted, disappointed with myself for breaking the long record of celibacy. Feeling tearful one morning, I clearly heard God's voice resonate within me, saying, "I understand your needs." I took this as confirmation of his approval, rather than simply hearing those words as the Lord's compassion, spoken in a consoling tone mingled with sadness.

God would have to literally "shake" me out of my self-deception. In the pre-dawn of Saturday morning, September 4, 2010, a powerful 7.2 quake struck forty kilometers from Christchurch. Our lives were turned upside down. The seismic activity continued daily, aftershocks by the score. During those uncertain months, I hung a Miraculous Medal around my neck after reading Mary's promise to St. Catherine Labouré to swiftly come to our aid, and each morning I prayed, just as she asked: "O Mary conceived without sin, pray for us who have recourse to thee. Sweet Mother, I place this cause in thy hands (three times)." By then, disquieted by the events around us, and weary of bargaining with God about my tendencies and needs, I became consumed by a fervent desire to revert to celibacy and to return to the sacraments of the Church.

I wept from time to time before the Lord in the Tabernacle and began to recall how wonderful it had once been to be so close to Jesus. I was regaining my spiritual eyes to see that homosexual sex was wrong. This conviction deepened, and I knew I needed help from above to somehow engineer such a life-changing choice.

When the second more deadly earthquake delivered its fearsome blow to Christchurch weeks later, an upward thrust two and a half times greater than gravity, the city was left in ruins with 185 people killed as buildings collapsed. Our home was unlivable for three weeks, trashed and without power or water. James stayed elsewhere temporarily; I joined an old friend in her undamaged apartment. It was Lent. I knew what I must do. After a six-year relapse, I was filled with nervous apprehension as I approached the confessional. My voice suddenly choked with emotion, I unburdened my sins to the priest and repented. That was it. No turning back now, ever again. The next day, it seemed as though years had fallen from me like scales. It is difficult to describe or explain this sense I had of feeling lighter, younger, spiritually renewed and somehow returned to an earlier state of soul. I broke out in smiles. It felt so amazingly good to be pure, to be chaste, to recover my innocence through absolution.

The decision to reinstate celibacy was an option James had always made provision for in the initial terms of our relationship. Although surprised and a little wounded at first, he met this news with exceptional understanding and with a maturity that has left me grateful, relieved, and full of admiration. James and I remain close companions who still share the same home, and he continues to accept and encourage me in this fuller commitment to my Catholic faith. No longer hampered by compromises or excuses, I can embrace life and the sacraments now with a clear conscience.

Such a tremendous amount of healing has gone on for me in the innermost parts of my being over the past two decades. Ten of those years were spent in counseling therapy, where the core of my problems began to unravel. First my father's death, then my mother's, also brought a degree of closure. Of course, the mainstay of my healing process has been the sanctifying graces available through the Lord's living legacy to Holy Mother Church: in the sacraments, most especially the Eucharist.

True healing began for me with the honest realization and admission that my inclination to same-sex attraction was, and is, "intrinsically disordered," just as the Church in her wisdom teaches. This truth has increased in clarity over time, as the Divine Physician has restored order to my heart and mind. None of this means, of course, that I, myself, am intrinsically disordered. In fact, today I know that I am, indeed, a new creation: more of a pilgrim than a prodigal, a happier and more integrated person, with a deep sense of peace that other people seem to notice.

A friend of mine surprised me recently by saying, "You are such a great inspiration to people!" I told him I had no idea. It never occurred to me. He wanted to understand what made me so committed to my faith, but a precise answer to this is difficult to pinpoint. I guess that when you've lived to the full all that the world has to offer—all the devil's false promises—and then come to experience the Lord's saving love, everything changes. I now know beyond all doubt that I am greatly loved by him— and that is the most wonderful knowledge in the world! I am not some hapless microbe awash in an evolutionary void!

I see evidence of God's presence and providence, signs of his infinite care and attention in so many details of my day-to-day life, and therefore I feel a security and contentment I've never known before. My house is built solidly on the Rock, which is Christ and the foundation of the Church given to Saint Peter. I start every day thanking Jesus for so many, many things. "What return can I make to the Lord for all that he gives me?" (Psalm 115:12).

Prayer has a special priority for me. I mean, spending time with the one you love is so important, so I get up early and sit for an hour in the company of Jesus before the day begins, and several times a week I try to make a Holy Hour of adoration along with Mass.

Mary also occupies a special place in my heart as my spiritual Mother, and in following the guidelines laid down by her at Medjugorje, I'm invested with the armory needed to keep me constant in faithfulness and chastity: I pray the Rosary daily, study the Scriptures, go to regular Confession (weekly now), receive Jesus in Holy Communion frequently, and I fast two days a week. Most months, I keep the First Saturday devotions requested at Fatima.

In recent times, I was able to satisfy a burning desire to make pilgrimages to holy sites in honor of Our Blessed Mother: first to Fatima and Garabandal, then Lourdes, and finally to Medjugorje, where I received a calling to the Franciscan Order. Two years after returning home, I was professed as a Lay Franciscan.

Today, my children are all adults and successful in their chosen fields. I recall Nathan reassuring me several years ago, "I know you worry, Dad, but all your kids love you very much." Maybe the steady foundation we had together, when all four children were young, has helped enormously. Back then I spent so much time initiating entertainment, taking them trekking and camping overnight, going to football with the three boys, doing fun things together, hardly ever missing my nightly bedtime round of reading to each child individually. Since the marriage break-up, I have always tried to be supportive in their lives and activities. When the youngest of my sons experimented with drugs in his late teens, I was able to be there with him every day of his recovery program and through his ongoing difficulties, which has made us very close. Now there are four delightful grandchildren who bring added pleasure as the family circle widens.

As for Anna and me, we maintain a good relationship. I can still hear her saying to the family-court counselor during our formal separation, "Part of the sadness of parting, for me, is that I will lose my best friend." Twenty-eight years have intervened since that painful period, and time has done wonders for both of us. The fact that we have always communicated well, kept in touch as the children grew up, has helped in the process I'm sure. We have long chats fairly frequently, heart to heart, eye to eye, about matters of paramount concern as well as the laughable peculiarities of the world and human nature.

Like Saint Paul, I can say, "Although I have been a blasphemer, a persecutor and a rabid enemy, he took mercy on me because I did not know what I was doing when I opposed the faith" (Timothy 1:12-13). The bramble thicket, that area of my psyche I have continuously wrestled with, guards me against the danger of spiritual pride, and I am the freest I've ever been—no longer governed by my body's appetites, no longer weighed down by secrets, old baggage or guilt. The profoundly destructive effects of rejection, which got me into so much trouble in the past, the craving for love and a need to belong, don't snare me in their sticky webs. The old black dog has been chained for two decades and no longer overshadows my thoughts and spirit.

I am nearing seventy now, and the Lord has kept me fairly youthful in spirit and body. Since I surrendered fully to Him, He has lavished extraordinary graces to help with my decision for chastity and has fostered a stability in me I could never have imagined. I look back at all the lives which used to be me—several lifetimes, really, and I marvel at how mightily I have been blessed, how I have been transformed by an ever-deepening intimacy with the God of love who is as close to me as my own heart. In him, I belong.

Amazingly, a personal prophecy was given to me several years ago by a friend: "The Lord is giving back to you the years the locusts have devoured" (Joel 2:25). That time is now.

SIX

Marital Hell to Marian Bliss

EVERYTHING CHANGED FOR US when my father, David Leatherby (I'm his namesake), got a new job in California and met his new boss. Burt Bride was his name, and Dad admired him greatly. Sitting down at the dinner table after a long day's work at his new job, my father would tell me and my siblings true tales about the virtues, honesty, and courage he saw in Mr. Bride, the western regional manager for Safeway stores, with only a sixth-grade education. There was only one unfortunate thing about Burt Bride—he was Catholic—and we Leatherbys had been breathing anti-Catholicism like air, as did all of our devout Methodist relatives from our home state of Bible-Belt Iowa.

One day, Mr. Bride called my father into his office. Dad's first thought was, "Uh oh, I'm going to get fired." Mr. Bride skipped past any small talk and said to him bluntly, "We may leave here and never be friends again, but I'm willing to take that chance. Have a seat." Dad sat down as relaxed as a sprinter at a starting block. "David, I just want you to know that I'm Roman Catholic, and I represent the one true faith. The Catholic Church is the one that Jesus started, and it has the fullness of truth. If you can prove me wrong, I'll quit the Catholic Church and become a Methodist. But if I prove I'm right, you have to become a Catholic. Do we have a deal?" He extended his hand toward my father, a headstrong and intractable man, who was never one to back down from a challenge.

"Okay," my dad countered, "you've got a deal."

Mr. Bride handed him some spiritual reading: *The Story of a Soul* by St. Therese of Lisieux and *The Confessions of St. Augustine*—both written by Doctors of the Church, and *The Imitation of Christ* by Thomas à Kempis. Literature like this my dad hadn't found in any Protestant denomination. Imbued with such profundity of love and faith, these writings made him feel that he had been missing something in his life. He grew convinced that there was something far deeper, greater, more sublime and mystical to Christianity than what he had known. God was so much more than he had ever realized. When he shared his insights with my mother, she protested immediately, but then secretly researched Catholicism on her own. Each of my parents came to the conclusion in a few short months that they desired to enter the Catholic Church.

I was only ten years old, the oldest of five children, and when Dad announced to me, "I want you to know that we're becoming Catholic," I threw a formidable fit. The only Catholicism I'd been introduced to was a strange Catholic couple down the street whose three kids were "total nerds." Running back to my bedroom, I flopped on my bed and wailed, "I don't want to be a Catholic! I don't want to be like *those* people!"

A few months after Mr. Bride's challenge, our entire family was conditionally baptized into the Catholic Church on December 22, 1965. Back then, baptism was required in case our original baptism was invalid. "You will be going to a Catholic school," announced my father. In the span of one day, I fell from being a bright star among public-school friends to a lonely, inadequate newbie. And there was the Mass. What the heck was everyone saying, and why were they doing calisthenics in the pews? My parents also signed me up to be an altar boy for the Latin Mass. Disoriented and adrift on the altar, I wandered through alien territory among strange rituals in a dead language. Meanwhile, my anti-Catholic relatives kept chirping surreptitiously in my ear, "Don't you know that the Catholic Church will lead you to hell? They pray to saints, they worship idols, and they think the pope is God! Why did your parents do this?"

Well, my parents never looked back and went on to become "even better Catholics" by having five more children. They sent all ten of us to Catholic grammar schools and Catholic high schools. Even so, my siblings and I became products of North American culture, showing up for Sunday Mass when it didn't get in the way of our plans, and selectively deciding which parts of our faith were worthy of belief and which were destined for a spiritual dumpster. For most of us Leatherbys, it was okay to call ourselves Catholic and decide for ourselves what Catholicism was.

When I was sixteen, I attended a play on a small stage surrounded on three sides by an audience of school members, some of whom were from the neighboring Catholic girls' school. During the play, a fourteen-year-old girl, who was facing me in the seats across the way, caught my eye. She had an innocence and a purity about her that attracted me—and she was pretty. I started waving to her. Then I waved again . . . and again. In her shyness, she didn't know what to make of me. As soon as the actors took their bows, I walked up to her and introduced myself. I found out her name was Jennifer and never did find out what the play was about.

Three years later, we married at the tender ages of nineteen and seventeen. In our first eight years of marriage, my wife and I had four children—Kimberly, Jeremy, Katie, and Matt—and to provide for them, I set my sights firmly on being successful in the world. Working like a slave to mammon, I founded two businesses: first, a painting contracting company, and then a retail appliance store, which grew to five storefronts. Upon selling these businesses, I went into partnership with my dad and founded a chain of ice cream parlors called Leatherby's Family Creamery. Franchises opened up quickly throughout Northern California, Nevada, Utah, Arizona, and Florida. We ended up selling over thirty franchises and became known as the hottest food franchise in the United States. My dad was even invited to be on the iconic *Tonight Show Starring Johnny Carson* to tell his success story, but he declined because he was selling franchises as fast as he could talk to people and felt the national exposure would overwhelm him.

Life seemed perfect. I had it made: a classy home, a beautiful wife, money, four great kids, and a Cadillac with a phone in it (which was almost unheard of at the time). But I still felt I was lacking something. One day, I picked up and flipped through our Sacramento Catholic newspaper (my dad had everything Catholic splayed across his desk). When I came across a write-up about a five-day silent retreat, I felt a tug in my heart and decided to go—an odd decision at age twenty-eight, considering silence was foreign to me. I always had something to say. On my first day, I began to sweat from the strain, but I did keep my mouth shut, except to speak during a spiritual direction hour each morning, when I met with a Jesuit priest.

In this unfamiliar school of silence, grace began to stir my conscience, and I turned my attention inward. I had to admit to myself that when it came to my faith, I was really a lukewarm Protestant, disguised as a Catholic—a man who, helped along by my suspicious relatives, felt that the Church was an old-fashioned inflictor of arbitrary rules dictated by old, uninformed men in Rome. Other than sitting in a pew with my family most Sundays and getting my kids to say an occasional half-hearted prayer at bedtime, I had not nurtured myself or my family with the Catholic faith. As a result, my moral character was punctured with holes that I was seeing for the very first time. "What kind of person am I?" I asked. The answer came. While I appeared to place others before myself—my wife, my kids, my friends, even strangers—everything was ultimately about my desires, my prestige, my pleasure, power, and possessions. To get my way, I was a person of compromise, someone who could twist the truth without a prick of guilt. I was selfish. I was duplicitous. In fact, I began to feel dirty.

As I persevered through my silent scrutiny, God brought me closer and closer to him, to the point that by the fifth day, I could think a question and the Lord would answer—not with a clear or audible voice, but through my knowledge of his response. Such spiritual communion had never happened in my life, and soon I didn't want the retreat to end.

On the last day, when I was kneeling in the retreat house chapel, I noticed an elderly nun, about eighty-five years old, praying in the front pew, and I thought to myself, "I bet she's done one hundred times more good in her life than I have in mine." Then another thought came: "Since I've never fully given myself to God and others, and I've only been truly saintly for a collective total of about one day, that would therefore mean that she only spent one hundred days doing good. But she's probably done one thousand times more good than I've ever done. . . but that would only be about three years of her doing good. My gosh, she's undoubtedly been a source of goodness for at least fifty years. That means that she's done twenty thousand times more good than I have!" Crumpling forward in my seat, I began to sob. I had never done anything that I felt made the world a better place. My whole life had been focused on me and what I wanted. "What will I say to God when I see him face-to-face?" In the crucible of silence, a cry rose from my heart: "Dear Lord, help me to be a better person. I want to make a difference in this world."

Those words became my daily prayer, and soon afterward, the Leatherby's Family Creamery franchise started to have business troubles. A franchisee in Florida had not paid his rent, and our company had guaranteed the lease. Since Florida law allows a landlord to sue for the full term of the lease and file an automatic judgment, we were hit with a judgment for $2,500,000, and that was only the beginning. Five lawsuits descended on us all at once. We had sold franchises to people who had decided to syndicate, who sold shares to hundreds of people who wanted to buy into Leatherby's franchises. So when things fell, a suing frenzy descended upon us.

I was in court at least every other day, accosted by attorneys who accused me, my father, and the entire Leatherby family of being a horde of cheats and frauds. They weren't searching for the truth; they were looking to win in order to crush us. Before then, I had thought lawsuits were about justice; but these were about lies, undue punishment, and stealing people's assets. Dad and I were being sued for whatever a person could be sued for. We were even accused of violating the federal RICO Act, which was used to prosecute gangsters in the Mafia. Sitting in court, day after day, I felt so angry that I often came close to throwing up. "I'll never escape this nightmare," I feared. "If I can't prove I'm innocent, the end of this could be prison."

Almost daily, for months, our personal names were smeared across the local newspapers. Much of Sacramento knew the ignominious name of Leatherby and believed every line they read. I lost many of my friends and became a person of ill repute. Even in church, I could hear people whispering my name.

My father lost his home. I couldn't keep mine either. We lost the business and had to file bankruptcy. Mom and Dad were able to keep ownership of our one ice cream parlor in our hometown, but almost all the money from the store had to be pledged to pay our legal fees. I moved my family into an apartment, and the company that bought the franchises hired me for six months to help with the transition. But when that ended, the money ran out.

I kept myself going by repeating, "At least I have my family. At least I have my health." At night, for recreation and to help relieve stress, I would play full-contact flag football, and during a game, my leg was dislocated and my knee so severely damaged that it had to be reconstructed with plates and screws. All my life, I'd been an athlete who loved sports, and now I would never run, or jump, or play sports again.

"Oh Lord," I prayed, "what could be worse than all this?"

My wife, Jennifer, approached me shortly thereafter and said, "You know what? I don't think I love you anymore. I don't want to be married to you. This is no fun. Our names are splattered across the papers, we're being humiliated, and you're not the same person I married. You're not happy."

Despairing and dejected, I reluctantly assented to moving away from my wife and four kids, wondering if my heart could bear the load. I had no job, no money, and was on crutches. I felt terrified. Borrowing a few bucks, I moved myself into a flophouse downtown and lived on the fourth floor because it was the cheapest one. To get to my room, I had to crawl over prostitutes and drunkards passed out on the stairs, and hobble down the hallway of a floor filled with sex, drugs, and abuse. At night, the sounds of sin would pass through my paper-thin walls.

God broke me. I look back and can see his methodical hand as, one after another, he separated me from my idols: my good name, my friendships, my money, my possessions, my health, even my family—everything in which I had placed my trust without realizing it. In order for my soul to survive, I had to find a new source of strength: something that would never leave me—something eternal that I could trust and believe in—something that would love me unconditionally. If I did not find it, my heart was destined to give into darkness, which it almost did.

Bitterness came knocking, and I welcomed it in. I felt I had a right to thoughts of rage, revenge, and impurity. Because I didn't like people or trust them anymore, I used them in superficial friendships and again began to justify twisting the truth to get what I wanted. My new close friends became alcohol, profanity, and plenty of blame. But in my brewing anger, I never did get upset with God. I didn't want to, although great doubts and painful questions about his faithfulness plagued my mind: "Why did you abandon me? Where were you? Where are you?"

My heart felt alive only toward my children. Every Sunday morning, I would pick them up and take them to church, or pop in for a weekday-night visit to put them to bed, even though Jennifer would dash away when I came anywhere near her. I had lost hope that she would ever love me again. She had abandoned me in my time of trial and acted so hateful and angry toward me that I didn't think I could ever trust her. Still, I desired my wife's affection and desperately yearned to return home. I wanted my family, and my kids needed their mom and their dad. Stumbling forward in a dimly lit faith, my new daily prayer became, "Dear Lord, help me get my family back."

Penniless, I set my sights on working for a particular commercial real estate company, which was the best in the nation. I must have called the hiring manager at least one hundred times, but he would never call back. I sat in the lobby of his office building at least ten times, but he would always walk on by. My last name wouldn't let me in the door. One day, I decided to be even more forceful and try to knock the door down. Hobbling into to his office on my three "legs," I said to his secretary, "Please tell Mr. Smith I'm here for my appointment" (which I didn't have).

"Sorry, sir. I don't see you on the books here."

"Oh, that must be a mistake. He's expecting me, and it's urgent."

The man came running out and upon seeing me, asked, "Do we have an appointment?"

"Yeah, we have an appointment to meet today."

"Are you sure?"

"I'm here, and I'd like to meet with you. Can we meet?"

Guilt must have gotten the better of him because he had me follow him into his office, where I nervously sat across from him and his imposing desk. I knew I had one shot, and I aimed high: "Mr. Smith, I've been successful at everything I've done in my life. What you read in the papers isn't all true. I promise you that I will be your top salesman. If I'm not in your top ten in the first year, you can fire me. Actually, I'll quit. You won't have to fire me. I promise you will never regret hiring me."

To my astonishment, he said: "All right, I'm going to make an appointment to give you a personality and aptitude examination, which includes math and communication skills, in order to assess your suitability for this work."

It was an eight-hour test. Afterward, he called me in to review the results and told me there was one area of concern, which might preclude him from hiring me: "You don't like doing detailed work. You're extremely low in your score here, and with this job, if you aren't a detail person, you can be sued and get into trouble. I'm not sure I should hire you."

Knowing my future and my family's survival depended on my response, I summoned all my strength: "Mr. Smith. Number one, you don't want a bookworm and a detail person to do this. You want a person who is going to create business and make things happen. I will do that. And number two, you want a person who knows their weaknesses. I spend one day a week catching up on all the detail work of my life so I'm sure to get it done because I am aware that I don't like it."

Looking up at me, he said, "Okay, you're hired. You can start when you're off the crutches."

"No," I responded. "That would be in four months. I need to start now." He reluctantly agreed.

"By the way," I added, "can you pay me a little?"

"This job is 100 percent commission. I can't give you enough to support a family."

"How much can you loan me?"

Mr. Smith, the regional manager, offered to loan me $2,500 a month for twelve months, barely enough to keep myself and family alive, supplementing Jennifer's meager income from working at the restaurant. Pressed against the wall, I had no choice but to succeed.

In commercial real estate, it takes about a year to generate an income. Without the luxury of being able to learn over a long period of time, I put every moment and ounce of energy allotted to me into becoming a successful commercial real estate broker. I got myself up at four in the morning and drove through town to memorize Sacramento's commercial real estate properties. With the scant money left for me at the end of each month, I ate only liquor-store peanuts, chips, and Snickers®, and lost a lot of weight. I was working eighteen-hour days, stopping at 10 or 11 p.m. and sleeping four hours a night, all in the hope that I might be able to earn my way back to my family. When I wasn't working, I was visiting attorneys or sitting in court, in a quagmire of acrimony. In short, I was in hell.

One day, when I stopped by the family apartment, Jennifer prepared to bolt, like usual, and as she turned her back to me, I said, "You look really unhappy. You just seem like you're so full of hatred toward me."

She spun quickly around and glowered at me with an icy stare. "Why wouldn't I be?" Then she erupted into tears. For the very first time, I saw my wife's vulnerability and pain. From within her came a paroxysm of deep, guttural sobs. "You've hurt me," she cried. "You've hurt me so badly."

Suddenly, Jennifer became a different person in my eyes. Through the crack in her armor, God gave me a grace, and it cut my heart to the quick. For the very first time, I saw her as his little child, as an anguished little girl, and I realized that all my years of selfishness, which I had thought were simply normal living, had hurt her in so many ways. Before then, I had blamed Jennifer entirely for her behavior and wondered, "Why won't she stand by me, like a good wife should? Why can't she understand why I'm miserable and grumpy?" I felt like she had abandoned me in the darkest moments of my life. I had been completely blind to my part in her pain. But at that moment, I saw how I had crushed and wounded this little flower, and all I could think of was, "What have I done? What have I done?"

After that, Jennifer's hatred for me remained, but a door in my heart had opened, which spurred me to try and help my wife even more. Eventually, money started coming in, not just out. After my first year of working in commercial real estate, there were two people vying for top rookie salesman in the Western region: myself and another man. Mr. Smith, my boss, was ecstatic with my performance. I was able to pay back his loans and had some money left over to put down on a deposit for a house for Jennifer and the kids—an old, cheap, run-down, three-bedroom fixer-upper.

Eventually, Jennifer allowed me to move back in because she loved her children who were crying out for their dad. My kids were overjoyed, and I received a capricious welcome from my wife who gave me permission to sleep in a different room or on the couch. To keep her from kicking me out again, I feigned a happy countenance, while suppressing deep resentments that had settled in my spirit: grudges against her, the opposing attorneys, the people suing me—the world.

Finally, an end came to the courtroom visits. In sum, Dad and I had to pay out about $1,500,000 in legal fees to clear our family name. After three years and thirty lawsuits, we never lost a single case; but to defend ourselves, it cost us everything we had. Among the many lawsuits and the lawyers spouting evil accusations and contrived threats, one attorney towered above them. The venom that surged from his mouth was so vicious and dishonest that, at times, I entertained creative ways to knock him off.

One day, when I was standing in a closing elevator where I worked, a hand reached in to stop the doors. When they re-opened, I was face-to-face with the nefarious attorney. He walked in. The doors closed. My first thought was insane: "Is God allowing me the opportunity to get even with this guy?" I instinctively froze and didn't say a word, like a cat bristling near its prey. As we ascended to one of the top floors, he turned to look at me and said, "You're Dave Leatherby," and he stretched out his hand. I wouldn't shake it. "I just want to tell you how much respect I have for you and your family. Through all of those trials, you kept your integrity. And those clients whom I represented . . . they were so evil . . . but I just want to let you know how I much I respect you." While he didn't own up to his role in the matter, his words nevertheless made him very human.

Stunned by his kindness, I reached out my hand to shake his. In that moment, I felt all the enmity I'd reserved specifically for him leave my heart.

My bad habits didn't all go away after I'd moved back home. On Friday nights, for instance, I often stopped into a bar downtown to have a few beers before going home. One evening, I noticed an acquaintance of mine, a successful attorney named Sam. He looked like he had been sitting in that bar since it had opened. I'd heard that he had left his wife. Now he was going through a divorce and losing touch with his kids. Carousing and drinking away his days, he was careening along a downward spiral. That day, Sam was flirting with all the women in the bar, and his face appeared sad and drawn. My heart stirred with compassion because I imagined myself just steps away from landing in his shoes. "At least I'm better off than this poor guy," I thought.

A couple of months later, when I was sitting by the side of a pool, watching my kids race at a recreational swim meet, a man walked up to me whom I didn't recognize. He had a celestial glow about him and the most peaceful, content, carefree, joyful look on his face that I'd ever seen. Then it hit me... "Sam, is that you? You look wonderful. You look terrific. How are you? What a change!"

"I've never been better in my entire life."

"Really? What makes you say that?"

"Can I ask you a personal question? Are you Catholic?"

"Yeah, I'm Catholic. Why?"

"Well, I took a pilgrimage. I went to this place called Medjugorje. Have you ever heard of Fatima?"

"Yes, I have."

"It's like that, but it's happening today, right now in our lifetime. The Blessed Virgin Mary is appearing to six young people in Yugoslavia." Then he began to share with me the conversions and the miracles he had witnessed: "Things are turning gold and the sun spins . . . I saw heaven touching earth and it changed my life."

I took a couple steps backward, worried I'd catch his crazy. "That's nice. I'm very happy for you," I sputtered and escaped as quickly as I could. Back home, I told my wife, "That poor Sam, he's lost it. His pendulum has swung from one side of kooky to the other."

Yet all week long, I couldn't stop thinking of the effervescent glow on his face. He looked about twenty years younger than the last time I'd seen him. He couldn't make that up. As the following Saturday approached, I began to anxiously await the chance to see him again. Once I arrived at the swim meet, I started running around looking for him but only found his son. "Is your dad here?"

"Oh yeah, he's right over there."

Rushing up to him, I said breathlessly, "Sam, you've gotta tell me more about these apparitions, this thing going on in Medjugorje."

Sam's mouth broadened into a contagious grin. Handing me a small pamphlet, he said, "I thought I might run into you today."

Sitting myself down on the grass, I devoured that pamphlet. Something long lost was stirring in my heart. It was hope. My mind raced with the question, "What if I had been alive two thousand years ago, and someone approached me to tell me about a man who was working miracles, who might be the Messiah? What would I have done? Would I have been a person to seek him out, to seek out the truth? Or would I have been one to say, 'Oh, that's nice. I have no need to find out. I'm fine with my life.'" I hoped I would have immediately gone to seek out Jesus. Within seconds, I knew I had to go to Medjugorje.

Challenged and inspired, I went home and suggested to my wife, "Let's take a vacation."

"Well," she retorted, "I don't want to go to some Communist country. That's nuts. Let's go somewhere fun like Hawaii."

"But I really want to go to this place."

"Fine, just go then."

My new prayer of earnest became, "I want to know the truth. Is the Mother of God really appearing in Medjugorje? And what's more. . . is the Catholic faith true?" Only a week later, in July of 1990, I found myself on an airplane, coping with various fears: "Dear Lord, I'm not trying to worship Mary. Really. I just want to know what's real. I don't mean to offend you." I was afraid not only of the mutterings from my anti-Catholic past, but also the whispers from myself: "If Mary is really appearing from heaven, that means I'm going to be in her presence, and she is goodness through and through. What might I look like in the light of such holiness?"

My first day in Medjugorje, I could tell immediately that I was in a spiritual oasis. Pilgrims were gathered from all over the world, cradled by an invisible mist of profound peace. Different races and nationalities were praying, singing, and worshipping God together with all their hearts. But after three days in Medjugorje, I grew utterly disappointed. I didn't just

131

travel halfway around the globe to find peace. I wanted to know the truth—whatever that was. Disconsolate, I went to the evening Rosary in St. James Church on my third night, and as I knelt next to an American pilgrim whom I'd befriended, I looked down and watched the silver chain of my rosary turn from silver to gold in front of my eyes. I was utterly amazed, but then my mind inserted skeptically, "Maybe they make trick rosaries over here, which change color with the heat of your hand or something." Pushing the rosary toward my neighbor, I asked, "What do you see? What color is this rosary?"

"Well, it's black."

"No, no, not the beads, the chain."

"It's gold."

Even then, I didn't believe a miracle had happened. "Maybe," I thought, "these communist countries have 'radiation leakage,' like in Chernoble." The next day, I came across a group of Americans and sidled up next to them to enjoy the sound of my native tongue. They were chatting about a private appointment with the visionary Marija at her home. Sensing my eager ear, one of them turned to me and asked, "Would you like to join us?"

"Oh, yes! I really would."

We walked across fields and in between rows of grapevines and came to stand in front of Marija's simple home, built of stone and mortar. "It is here," I thought, "that I'm going to find out the truth. I will scrutinize Marija—the way she's dressed, the way she speaks—and I'll be able to tell if she's a fraud, if she has ulterior motives or is in this for herself." When she walked out of her front door to greet us, the group of Americans began to take pictures of her, and she bowed her head forward. The interpreter said, "Marija asks that you put your cameras down."

"Silly Americans," I thought to myself. "What are you doing?" Then Marija lifted up her eyes with a look of gentle joy, peace, and love. I felt, at that moment, like she was looking straight into my soul.

She continued, "You didn't come here to take my picture. You came here to listen to Our Lady's words. "It is no accident that you are here. God is calling you, and God is real. . ." Members in the group pulled out their cameras, again, and started taking pictures of her. She put her head down, looking very sad, and waited. When the camera flashes ceased, she looked up at us, and then she shared some of the most profound wisdom I had ever heard—holy words that a saint might impart. Marija genuinely wanted us to hear and to follow Mary's messages. Clearly our understanding was deeply important to her. Not only was her sincerity manifestly apparent, but she had the same look on her face that Sam, my attorney friend, had: serenity, contentment, joy. "How often do you pray?" someone asked her.

She answered, "Well, I've offered my entire life as a prayer to God."

At that moment, I couldn't take any more honesty and wisdom, so I turned around and walked away. I believed this young woman. Her whole being exuded truth . . . therefore, I had to believe that Mary was actually coming to us from heaven . . . therefore, what Mary was saying was real, and her messages pointed to the truth of the Catholic Church. Confronted with the fact that I hadn't at all been living my Catholic faith, and thus the life God intended for me, an avalanche of shame, remorse, sorrow, and regret came crashing into my spirit, and I wanted to be alone. I'd grown up priding myself in being the only kid in school who never blubbered, and then the man of the house who never whimpered, and now I was convulsing with tears, as if my body couldn't vomit out my sins fast enough. Walking into the nearby village cemetery, relieved to find no one there, I fell to the ground, weeping profusely. I sobbed for two straight hours. I cried so hard that I couldn't stand up. The galling thought kept coming to my mind that if I were to die right then, the world would not be a better place because I had lived. In fact, I'd probably made it worse. "Forgive me, Lord!" I prayed. "If you want me to finally follow you, you will have to help me because I've broken every promise I've ever made. My every New Year's resolution has been a debacle . . . every diet lasts one day, so if you want me to be different, you'll have to change me."

On the remaining days of the trip, I walked buoyantly in the Spirit and encountered miracles and many wonderful people. When it came time to return to California, I didn't want to leave because I felt like I was already home. On the plane ride back, I knew that my life had changed forever for the better. Only one small worry nagged at my joy: "Lord, please don't make me a religious fanatic."

In the days following Medjugorje, I thought I was doing great. Every morning, I woke up filled with joy and peace. I loved my family more than ever, and I wanted nothing more than to pray and to study my faith. The Bible and the lives of the saints replaced my morning routine of the daily Sacramento Gazette. Friday nights, I skipped past the bar and prayed for my friends inside that they might come to know the truth and be filled with joy. God was more real to me than my own right hand, and the sins around me that I hadn't been able to see suddenly caught my attention and clashed with my spirit. When my kids would play certain movies at home, I'd gasp, "Why the heck are we watching this?" Certain television shows, books, and magazines lying around the home slowly found their way to the door, while the messages of Our Lady slowly found their way in. Mass became part of my daily routine; then I joined a Rosary group; then I started my own Rosary group, never insisting my family join me in anything. Life, for me, became wonderful. I was experiencing great peace and indescribable joy, resting in the assurance that my faith was true and that what I was doing was right.

In my family's opinion, I had indeed become a fanatic. To give you the view behind their eyes, I'll let my son Jeremy, who was twelve at the time, share his perspective. . .

After Dad went to Medjugorje, he was never the same. Only after he got back did my two sisters and my brother and I find out that he'd been on a pilgrimage, not a business trip. Something happened to him there. Dad became Mr. Catholic Church, and we kids rebelled against it. He smiled way too much.

My dad is strong and masculine, a real man's man. He raised my brother and me not to cry (my two sisters could, but not for long). We didn't fuss as kids because we'd get swatted. I felt intimidated by him, and at the same time, always longed for his embrace and his words of pride and unconditional acceptance. But that wasn't his way, nor the way of his father before him. Before his trip to Medjugorje, I'd never seen my dad get a misty eye, much less cry. But afterward, whenever someone would speak of Our Lady, I would see tears running down his cheeks. If the priest in the homily at Mass said simply, "And the Blessed Virgin Mary . . .," we kids, who normally weren't alert in church, would come to attention, look down the pew, and see Dad wiping his eyes at the sound of Our Lady's name. So I knew there had to be something special about the Mother of God. . .

My wife was mortified by the new me. I didn't want to go to the same social gatherings and parties. I cleaned up my speech. I refused to see my wife as an object of my pleasure, but as my complimentary partner by using natural family planning instead of artificial birth control. Catholicism, for me, was now God's plan for humanity's happiness and fulfillment, possessing a truth and wisdom different from the world's. No longer a bunch of burdensome rules with occasional benefits, it was life itself.

"You've lost it!" she'd holler at me.

"But I'm a better person," I tried to reassure her. Since Our Lady of Medjugorje was asking that we make holy objects and the Scriptures visible in the home, I displayed a Bible. Then when I went to hang a crucifix in a prominent place in our home, my wife stopped me: "People are going to think we're strange. You are not putting that in our living room!" Jennifer became so angry that just seeing a Miraculous Medal around my neck would cause her to snap, "Get that off! That's so embarrassing. What are people going to say?" The more happy and faithful I became, the more she hated me. Her ire progressed to the point that if I came close to her, she'd move away. If I touched her hand, she'd yank it back from me, even directly in front of others. It felt so painful. In time, she wouldn't even sit in the same room with me.

"Dear Lord," I'd pray. "Soften her heart. Help her to come to know the truth." But time only made her worse. "What is happening? Why can't she see that the new me is improved?" All who knew my wife would have said she had a naturally sweet disposition, but one day, in particular, it left her. I was standing in our bedroom walk-in closet when she stormed in, swearing and roaring with such fury that I felt myself tremble. It seemed as if someone had taken over my wife's body: "Get rid of this religious stuff! Why are you going to Mass every day? You're pushing this on our children! All our friends are talking about you. I can't take it anymore!" Jennifer was petite at five feet-two and one hundred pounds; I was six feet tall and two hundred fifty pounds. Yet I was afraid of her.

Standing sheepishly in our closet entryway with my head down, I wondered, "Lord, have I done the wrong thing?" I had tried to be gentle and slow in my expression of the faith, but even so, the people closest to me knew I was different. "God," I asked, "do I save my marriage by burying my faith, though you will always know that in my heart I love you? Or do I continue doing what I feel is right?" I couldn't imagine not openly

135

practicing Catholicism and hiding my most cherished beliefs, and yet I was making my wife miserable. The thought came to me, "Perhaps God wants me to live alone for the rest of my life. Maybe I need to accept this as my suffering, as a penance for the sins of my past." So I began to say a new prayer, "Dear Lord, not my will but yours. If you want me to be alone, I will be. I will never remarry and will support my wife for the rest of my life. Whatever you want, I accept. I trust in you." For the first time in my life, I truly let go in complete surrender.

Not long after that, my marriage, which had been in decay for seven years, deteriorated to the point that I resolved to give Jennifer her freedom. The day I arranged for divorce papers, my heart felt so heavy that I could hardly get to work. As I sat at my desk, I couldn't function, for all morning I knew that I was going to leave work at noon to pick up a document that would end sixteen years of marriage. At the close of the day, I would come home to my wife and say, "I do not believe in divorce, but here are your papers if you wish to sign them. You can have everything: custody of the kids, the house, my share in the restaurant, all the money, and your freedom. I don't want to make your life miserable. I'm so sorry. I just want you to be happy." I buried my head in my hands and broke out in a cold sweat. It was 9 a.m., and I couldn't imagine making it through the day.

Before me on my desk was a small statue of the Pietà, the image of Our Lord's crucified body lying across Mary's lap. Looking at her, I said, "Blessed Mother, if this is not God's will for my life, you have to intervene because I'm going to serve these papers to Jennifer." At that moment, the phone rang.

"Dave, this is Curtis from the prayer group."

I had seen Curtis at a prayer gathering I attended occasionally, and I didn't know him at all well.

"Curtis? What's this about?"

"Hey, uh, can I meet with you this morning?"

"No, sorry. Today is a bad day."

"Um . . . I'd really like to meet with you this morning. Do you have a few minutes?"

I didn't know the guy well enough to fathom why he was calling me.

"Today really isn't a good day," I reiterated. "What do you have in mind here?"

"I can't tell you."

Irritated, I stated, "You're going to have to tell me what this is about."

"Well," he said, "I have a message to give you."

"A message?"

"Well, there's a young girl in the prayer group we've attended, and she told me I had to give it to you this morning."

Curiosity got the best of me, and I agreed to meet with him—not anywhere I would be noticed. "I'll meet you at the park," I offered. Once there, I was greeted by a big teddy bear of a man, "Tell me, again, what happened," I urged.

"Well, I have a cousin in the prayer group, a twenty-one-year-old girl who has a special gift. Our Lady speaks to her heart, and last night she was awakened in the middle of the night and asked to take down this message for you. She was also told it had to get to you this morning." Then he handed me a plain, white, sealed envelope.

"A message for me? I don't even know her." Sitting down next to him on a park bench, I opened the envelope and pulled out the message. It read:

> My dear son, this is your Heavenly Mother. I am speaking to you through my servant. God has heard your "yes." He has suffered with you in your considerable pain, which will bear tremendous fruit. God has great designs for your life and your family, a plan to redeem and heal your marriage, and a plan to bring many souls to Christ through all of you. Heaven does not want your family separated. Do not give the papers to your wife. Have faith, and trust that everything is in my hands. You have given your life to me. You have consecrated your family to me, and they are mine. I will take care of them, and I will take care of you. Do not lose hope. Love. Believe. Put God in the first place, and I will be with you always until the end of time. I have placed something on my son's heart for you.

Tears begin to gush from my eyes. It was the most loving, wonderful, preciously beautiful letter from my heavenly Mother. In it were things that only God could have known about me. Suddenly, I had such hope. I believed with all my heart that things were going to be okay.

Clutching the letter, moistened by my teardrops, I reread it, savoring each word, and this time, the last line jumped out at me: "I have placed something on my son's heart for you." At first, I thought I needed to go to a Catholic church as soon as possible and kneel before the Blessed Sacrament to ask the Lord what was on his heart; so I folded up the letter, put it back in the envelope, and stood up to go. Then another thought came. Maybe the "son" Our Lady was referring to wasn't Jesus. "Curtis," I asked, "Is there anything more?"

Curtis stuttered and hesitated . . . "Well, uh, this might sound weird, but before I came here, I went to a chapel where I knelt down before a statue of Our Lady and said a prayer to her. At that moment, it felt to me like she placed something on my heart for you."

"What is that?"

"You're supposed to go tell your wife how much you love her."

"That's it?" I thought. "I've done that a million times." But because of the circumstances, I complied, believing I had to trust Our Lady was at work. Thanking Curtis profoundly, I left the park and drove immediately to Leatherby's Family Creamery in Sacramento, the one remaining store in the family business. Before I got out of the car, I called my attorney to tell him to tear up the divorce papers. Then, silently, I said, "Mother, even though I believe my wife's heart is dead toward me, I'm going to honor you, and out of obedience, do what you're asking of me." With trepidation, I walked into the restaurant. Jennifer was behind the cash register, managing the store.

"I have something to tell you."

"What?" she barked, refusing to look at me. "What is it?"

"Can I talk to you for a minute?"

"Does it have to be right now? I'm busy, and I don't want to see you."

"Please, humor me. Treat me like a human being." Begrudgingly, Jennifer stepped to the side of the store, faced me, and crossed her arms. Careful not to touch her, I turned to her and said," I just want you to know that you're the most important person in the whole world to me; I never want anyone else, and I will never be married to anyone else. Everything I have is yours, always, and I love you."

My wife's response was the silent stare of an ice queen—mean and hateful. She said nothing, and we parted ways as if I had given her a warrant for her arrest. As I walked back to my car, I noticed the sun fading behind the horizon, casting a bright orange, and yellow glow across the sky. Staring at the gentle beauty of the skyline, I cried out, "Mother Mary, how many times have I said similar words to her? Why did you ask me to do this again? You know it doesn't work!" Yet that wasn't entirely true, for unbeknownst to me, I had poured hot coals on Jennifer's head, and they started to burn.

Soon after that, a chain of terrible hardships struck my wife. One night, when she was shutting down the restaurant at closing time, two masked men with firearms stormed in and forced the eight people working as the closing crew to lie down on the floor. Jennifer was in the back room, counting the day's receipts. When she heard the commotion, she put the money on her chair and sat on it. The assailants found her and threatened to kill her if she didn't open the safe. Trying to be brave, she said, "No. I don't believe your guns have any bullets, and we worked hard for our money." Enraged, they grabbed her by the hair, threw her down, and shoved a gun in her face. At this, Jennifer lost control of her bowels and wet her pants, going into shock. Seeing the revealed money, the robbers then grabbed it and fled. After this traumatic experience, Jennifer was often overcome with fear for her safety. Her dreams were terrifying, and only with great difficulty could she return to work.

Only days later, my wife's brand-new, one-week-old status symbol was stolen right out of our driveway. She was going to be one of the "in moms," driving up to her kids' school in a big Suburban. And we hadn't bought car insurance yet. About a week after that, while Jennifer was sitting on the floor, letting our oldest daughter, Kimberly, curl her hair, she looked up behind her at the very moment that my daughter dropped the curling iron, which landed on Jennifer's eye. This left her in excruciating pain and concerned that her eye would go blind. One calamity after another occurred until she came to me one day and said, "I want to kill myself. When I drive around, I constantly think of driving into a telephone pole as fast as I can. I'm miserable. I hate my life. And you . . . you always seem to be so happy."

The only answer that came out of my mouth was, "You know, I receive great strength from going to Mass every day."

Despite my best efforts, things continued to deteriorate. On New Year's Day, the Solemnity of Mary, Mother of God, I stayed in the church after Mass to pray. Ever since my trip to Medjugorje, my eyes leaked, so I looked around to make sure no one was in the building. "Good," I thought, "I'm all by myself." And then the tears came in droves.

"Dear Lord, what's going on?" I prayed. "Why are all these problems happening? My wife is tormented. My family is miserable. Every single day, I've prayed for her. I've offered thousands of sacrifices for her, and now she wants to die. . . She says she wants to run her car into a . . ." All of a sudden, I felt a tap on my shoulder. A lady whom I'd never seen was standing right next to me, even though I had just looked around the church, and no one had been there. She smiled at me with great kindness and said, "All those problems that you're worried about, those are God's answers to your prayers." Then she turned around and walked out. "That's weird," I thought. "Who was she? And how could these bad things be God's answers?"

I didn't understand. The only way I could see my prayers being answered was in my beautiful children, not in Jennifer's trials and husband-directed religious persecution. My consolation came in noticing that, while she may not have been interested in the faith, my kids were taking to it. I often gave them things to read. I went into their rooms at night to pray with them. When their early teen years hit and they didn't always want to pray, I prayed out loud to God in front of them on their behalf: "Help my daughter (or son) become a great saint; help her (or him) to be strong and holy," and then I would trace the sign of the cross on their foreheads. At dinnertime, I'd always insert the subject of faith. When Lent came around in February, I asked my children as we sat around the table one evening, "What kind of sacrifices are you going to make for Lent?" I knew that question would set my wife off, but I took the chance.

Each of my kids announced what they planned to do: "I'm going to give up chocolate" . . . "I'm going to give up TV" . . . "I'm going to give up soda" . . . "I'm going to pray the Rosary every day."

"Well," my wife interjected, "aren't you going to ask me what I'm going to do?" I looked at her, agog, afraid to say anything. "I'm going to go to daily Mass," she stated.

Gripping my chair to keep from falling out of it, I responded calmly, "That's nice." Then I hesitantly ventured to ask, "Why daily Mass?"

"Because you're always happy no matter how badly I treat you."

Turning her toughness into determination, my wife went to Mass every single day in Lent, and as a result, joy entered her heart. She actually began to speak to me, and our relationship improved. The dark clouds that had followed her lifted, changing her entire countenance and causing the lines in her forehead disappear.

Come the end of Lent, I told my children, "There's a penance service tonight at the church, where priests will be available to hear Confessions and prepare us for Easter. Would you like to go with me?"

"We already went to Confession at school this week, Dad," answered my kids.

Then Jennifer, to my utter amazement, said, "I think I'd like to go." I don't think she had been to the Sacrament of Reconciliation since her very first and only Confession at age seven. I tried to act like this was normal. During the drive to church, I pleaded with God, "Please give my wife the strength to do this!" As she approached the confessional, her face turned pale, and she took a few deep, heaving breaths, as I held mine. When she sat down, face-to-face with a priest and her sins, she encountered a wonderful man, gentle and kind. When she was done confessing, he said to her, "God knows how hard it was for you to come in here. So for your penance, just say a single Hail Mary." She came out sobbing.

On the drive home, I mentioned, "You know, you've been given a great gift. Make sure you protect it because the devil will try to take away this peace that you have now."

She shot me a glare. "Why do you have to ruin everything?"

That night at 1 o'clock in the morning, Jennifer woke me up, yelling, "Someone is in the house! Someone is here! David, wake up. I heard the door slam. Someone is in the house!"

"I didn't hear anything, dear," I mumbled. Hysterical, she jumped up, turned on the lights, and without waiting for me, ran frantically through the house, opening doors and turning on all the lights. When she finally returned to our room, she sat on the edge of the bed, covered her face with her hands, and erupted in sobs.

I wanted to hold her but hesitated for fear of making things worse. "Do you want to tell me what's wrong?" I asked.

When she caught her breath enough to speak, she shared, "I had a dream. . . not one like I've ever had before. It seemed so real. I'm not sure it even was a dream. I was back in my father's house with my family. I walked outside into the backyard, which was beautiful. The sun was bright, the sky was blue and filled with white and fluffy clouds. Flowers were in bloom everywhere. I ran into my dad's bedroom, feeling so happy. Suddenly, I heard loud banging from outside his door. A hideous creature, ugly and gray with drawn skin, wanted in. It was—I couldn't tell if it was a man or a woman. I refused to open the door, but it kept on pounding with its fist, and I got so scared. . . I didn't know what to do. Then I heard a woman's voice: 'You have nothing to fear. Just pray.' There was a little, ceramic, white lamb on my father's nightstand, so I picked it up and held it to my heart. Then I started repeating, over and over, the words, 'Mary Had a Little Lamb.' Clutching the lamb in my hands, I had the courage to open the door and scream, 'Go away!' The creature reached out and tried to take the lamb away from me, but I wouldn't let go of it. At this, he grabbed the edge of the door, slammed it shut with a loud bang, and left. And that was the noise that woke me up."

The meaning of the dream, or vision, hadn't dawned on my wife until I explained its symbolism, which in fact, was reality. She had just gone to Confession, so she was "back in her Father's home," the Church, where the spirit is refreshed with life and joy and comfort. The devil was angry that he had been cast out and was trying to get back into her soul, his old home. But Our Lady spoke to protect her, calm her fears, and reveal the importance of prayer. When Jennifer prayed to Mary and embraced the lamb, who is Jesus, she had the courage and strength to send away the demon for good.

After Jennifer's confession, I could hardly believe the person who was my wife. She whizzed by me in the spiritual life and became a most wonderful partner, my best friend, and a fantastic mother. Together, we would invite forty to fifty people at a time to pray the Rosary or study the Bible in our home, which filled up quickly with religious paraphernalia. I had to tell my wife to quit buying pictures and statues of Jesus, Mary, and the saints. They were crowding the closets and stuffed under the beds. They were everywhere. It was embarrassing.

God was answering my prayers, one by one—prayers that came from the pit of my soul. I never believed that the flower I had crushed would blossom into fullness of life. First, the Lord had to soften my heart, and then he could enter my wife's. What it took for both of us was trials. He had to break us and strip us of all we thought gave us life, in order to save us. We couldn't see that God was all we needed until God was all we had.

At this point, the drama in my life switched from my wife to another member of my family. With Jennifer squarely "back in her Father's home," my second-eldest child, Jeremy, rose to the top of my prayer list. Jeremy was constantly pushing rules to their edge and quickly becoming my prodigal son. He was a great academic, a straight-A student, but ornery, always on the cusp of getting kicked out of high school. Physically small but tough, he played rugby and football hard and fast, and he drank so much beer that I gave him every kind of punishment I could think of. "This kid," I thought, "is never going to get it."

Here, in Jeremy's own words, is how the Blessed Mother intervened, once again, to change everything:

❧ ❧

My father often left religious things in my room, particularly books on the saints, and I wanted nothing to do with them. "Oh my gosh, Dad," I'd think, "get real," and I'd stick them unopened on the shelf. One spring day, when I was a sophomore in high school, I came home from rugby practice, and there was a book on my floor again. I rolled my eyes and picked it up. But this time I paused before sticking it on my shelf because on the front cover was an image of our Blessed Mother holding her infant Son. Because I saw Our Lady, I was interested.

I brought the book to my sister Kimberly who was two years older than I and had begun to open up to the faith. "What is this?" I asked. The book was called *Preparation for Total Consecration* according to St. Louis Marie de Montfort. Kimberly explained that a person says prayers in the book for thirty-three days and entrusts their lives to Mary in order to get closer to Jesus. At fifteen years old, I said, "I'm gonna do it. I'm going to give my life to Our Lady." It was a moment of incredible grace.

Looking back now, I think, "Holy cow! How did that happen?" My life was hardly virtuous. I was living in mortal sin by virtue of skipping Sunday Mass and knowing full well it was wrong; but I started to say the prayers of consecration, and every day I was faithful to it. One night after I had whooped it up, partying and drinking with my intoxicated friends, they all passed out. Sitting there in a stupor next to them, I pulled the little consecration booklet out of my overnight bag, and as I leaned over a garbage pail, in case I threw up, I said the prayers. "Mary," I began, and I started to cry. "I want to give my life to you. I know that I'm a wretched sinner and there's little hope for me, but please, please accept me."

When I turned sixteen, I discovered the brown scapular, a sacramental that the Blessed Mother gave to the Carmelite priest, St. Simon Stock, back in the year 1251. The scapular is made up of two, small, rectangular pieces of cloth from Carmelite habits, attached to a cord which goes loosely around one's neck. The piece that hangs in the front reads, ". . . a Sign of Salvation . . ." and the back piece says: "Whosoever dies wearing this scapular shall not suffer eternal fire." This promise holds if the person wears it in faith and trust. When I found out about the scapular, I gasped, "A free ticket to heaven!?" I would swim with it, shower with it. It never came off, even in the midst of my non-Christian life. In football practice, my front piece would sometimes poke out from my football chest pads, causing my buddies on the team to ask, "Hey, what's that hanging around you?"

"Oh, it's a scapular."

"A what?"

"Yeah, it's cool. The Blessed Virgin said that if you wear this, you're going to heaven." I had almost the whole football team wearing one.

One day that same year, a few of us on the team were working out in my garage. We were taking turns on our family weight machine, bench pressing one hundred and fifty pounds . . . one hundred eighty pounds. My dad walked in and said, "Let me try that. Put on all the weight that you can. I want to see if I can do it." My father is one of these guys who never works out. Every seven years, he goes on a workout kick that lasts all of two weeks. The weight bench was now set for two hundred and eighty-five pounds. I felt embarrassed: "There's no way. He doesn't work out." My dad lifted those weights eighteen times, like a freak of nature.

I feared my father, not just because he was big and strong, but because he was very strict, and I worried that I could never be good enough in his eyes. One day, I carried home a report card with a 4.6 grade point average. "I really knocked this one out of the park," I thought to myself. "Dad is going to have to be proud." As I stood in the sibling line, waiting for my turn to show him my grades, my pulse raced, my nerves danced, and I couldn't stop my body from fidgeting. Finally, my turn came. Dad took my report card into his hands, looked at it, paused and said, "Well, now I know what you're capable of."

"That's it? That's all he had to say?" My spirit was shattered, and I slunk away crestfallen. I still wonder if I might have toned down my bad behavior had my father lifted me up on his shoulders and paraded me around the house. I will never know. As it was, my wild antics continued and didn't die down until I went off to college at Notre Dame University in South Bend, Indiana, where my sister Kimberly was already a student.

There, I found a bunch of other Catholic students who were practicing the faith—and who were normal. I had assumed anyone who was really living his faith couldn't be cool. But thanks to Kimberly who had started a Rosary group that grew from five to three or four hundred people, including professors, staff, and sometimes the bishop, I gained many faith-filled friends. Alongside them, I started to go to Confession regularly and to openly live my Catholic faith.

When I came home for Christmas break, I prayed, "Lord, now that I'm here, I want to see if my conversion is authentic, so I'm not going to drink when I'm out with my friends" (which was all we ever did). I went to all the same party hangouts, but this time, I was the only one who was sober. Looking around, I thought, "Oh, my gosh! Was this really the way I was living my life? These people look ridiculous." It was then that I wondered, "Maybe God is calling me to do something different. Maybe he's calling me to something unique, something more."

Six months into my first year at Notre Dame, I decided to renew my consecration to Mary. On the campus stands a replica of the Lourdes Grotto in France, and I knelt there each day, for thirty-three days, to recite the prayers. After I had prayed the last words of consecration, I looked up at the statue of Our Lady in the cove and my heart spoke to her: "Throughout these thirty-three days, it's been placed on my heart very strongly that I am called to be a priest. . . Mary, is that true?"

For the first time in my life, I heard a voice within me that was not my own. The voice was Our Lady's, and she said just one word: "Yes." Along with her came an indescribable peace that flooded and pulsated through me from head to toe. For days to come, I was on fire with the Holy Spirit, praying all day and throughout the night. I don't know if I slept at all. Ever since then, I haven't doubted for a moment that I am called to be a priest.

$$\gamma \circ \quad \circ \gamma$$

One day I picked up the phone. It was Jeremy and he said, "Dad, don't renew my tuition next year. I'm not going to come back."

"Oh, no," I thought to myself. "He's gotten himself kicked out." I said, "But you worked so hard to get there. What's the problem?"

"I know that I'm supposed to be a priest."

145

I was already sitting down but felt like I had to sit down again. Even though I'd raised my kids in what may have seemed to some like an overly religious household, I'd never forced religion or religious vocations on my children in any way, neither had Jennifer. We'd never even spoken to Jeremy about becoming a priest. "You know, Jeremy," I said, "let's make sure it's the right thing to do. I'm going to pay your deposit for next year, and you and I will spend the summer visiting seminaries." He had no idea about different orders, much less seminaries, and neither did I. At the end of a summer of search and discovery, Jeremy signed up to be a priest for the Diocese of Sacramento and entered St. Charles Borromeo seminary in Philadelphia.

In the Jubilee year 2000, Jeremy and I, with Kimberly, who was now studying at the International Theological Institute in Gaming, Austria, decided to travel to Rome. There, we did what all the other faithful Catholics in Rome were doing that year, going from basilica to basilica, getting plenty of plenary indulgences. We had a marvelous time walking a seventeen-mile pilgrimage to pray at the designated Holy Doors of all the basilicas and churches, which St. Pope John Paul II had opened in celebration of the Jubilee year. We were enjoying ourselves so much that we ended up staying in Rome from Sunday to Sunday, longer than we had planned. The following Monday morning, Kimberly had to return to school in Austria, so Jeremy suggested, "Let's make the most of this trip. We'll drive all Sunday night from Rome to Kimberly's school near Vienna. Dad and I will switch off driving, and Kimberly will sleep in the backseat, so she can be awake for her classes tomorrow." Thus we began a twelve-hour drive through the night.

Still jet-lagged from the time change and tired from our whirlwind pilgrimage, I hopped in the driver's seat. Every two hours, Jeremy and I took turns driving our rental minivan. At 2 a.m., Jeremy said, "Dad, I can't go any further," so I took the wheel again as he reclined without a seatbelt in the front passenger seat. After a half hour, I started to doze off, so I opened my window to the freezing cold, October night air. The wind whipped my senses awake as we cruised along the fast lane of an autobahn at one hundred miles per hour. At 3 a.m., I saw a sign a couple hundred yards up the road, which read: "Vienna: 20 kilometers." We'd almost reached our destination. I breathed a sigh of relief, exhaled, and fell asleep.

Twenty seconds later, I opened my eyes. Just a few feet in front of me loomed the back lights of an eighteen-wheeler semi-truck. I slammed on the brakes and turned the wheel. It was too late. My head crashed into the windshield, cutting my chin wide open, as the back right corner of the truck smashed through the front windshield on the passenger side. The car spun 180 degrees and landed on the center divider, facing the oncoming traffic of the fast lane. I heard Kimberly saying calmly, "Dad, what just happened?" and then I blacked out.

When I came to, I asked in a daze, "Are you okay?" Kimberly had been lying down, and her body had simply hit the seats two feet in front of her. She was unharmed. Jeremy was moaning, "Oh, Dad. Oh, Dad." I looked over to my right. The corner of the truck had smashed Jeremy's face and sliced it from the middle of his nose down to his neck. His teeth were hanging down outside of his face, and his right eye had disappeared into his cheek. My beautiful son was so torn apart and disfigured that he looked like a scene from the movie, Alien, when the alien's face was opened in two. So much blood was pouring out of his head that I thought, "Oh, dear God. He's going to bleed to death. I've killed him!" Jeremy reached up his hand, and I said, "No, don't touch your face."

All of a sudden, a car zoomed by at over a hundred miles per hour, missing us by an inch. "If I don't get him to the side of the road," I thought, "we'll all die before I get him to a hospital." I opened the door quickly on my side and ran around to Jeremy's door, but it was smashed shut and wouldn't budge. So I climbed on top of the front of the car and reached through the shattered windshield to break out the remaining glass. Wrapping my arms around Jeremy's bloody body, I pulled him out and heaved him over my shoulders, as cars continued to fly by.

Sitting down in the middle of the median at night, I cradled Jeremy in my arms, like I did when he was a little child. I wished so desperately that he had been knocked out, but he kept talking: "What happened? I'm hurting, Dad. I'm hurting. It hurts . . . it hurts." Our surroundings were snowy, bitterly cold, and pitch dark, but for the headlight streaks of passing cars. I didn't know where we were—somewhere in Austria—in the middle of nowhere. I had no cell phone and no idea where to look for help, and I didn't speak German, the official language of Austria. Never in my life had I felt so helpless and so alone. As I sat there, holding my son close, he asked me, "Dad, can I die? Can I die now?"

"No. Jeremy, you've always been small, but you were the toughest kid on the football team," I told him. "Now you're going to have to be stronger than ever. We're going to pray. We're going to ask Our Lady and

147

all the saints to pray for us and help us." I didn't know what else to do. So we prayed, and a tremendous peace came over me. Somehow, I knew that everything was going to be all right, that even if he died, it was okay because "God is God, and I'm not. He knows all, and he has a plan." Amidst this penetrating sense of peace, I felt an unspeakable intimacy with Mother Mary holding her Son after he came down from the cross.

Suddenly, my daughter Kimberly ran across the freeway, and I worried that she would get hit. On the other side of the road, she started waving her hands, trying to flag someone down. We were in the middle of Austria, still one hundred and fifty kilometers from Vienna, and we didn't speak the language. "Even if someone does stop," I thought to myself, "are they even going to be able to speak English?"

A car caught sight of Kimberly and pulled over. With Jeremy in my arms, I ran across the freeway. A big, tall, handsome, blond-haired man got out of the car, and the first words from his mouth in a thick German accent were, "Can I help you?"—in English.

"How could he know to speak to us in English?" I wondered. The man asked what happened, and I told him, "We need to get my son to the hospital right away. I'm afraid he's going to bleed to death." Jeremy's entire body was shaking. He was going into shock.

"Put him in the front of my car. I'll turn the heater on," said the stranger.

Blood was everywhere, so I warned him, "He'll bleed on your car."

"It's okay," he responded, as if it was no matter. Then he opened his trunk, pulled out a blanket, put it over Jeremy, and turned on his car heater full blast. Whipping out his cell phone, he called for help immediately. Turning to Kimberly, I said, "Please be with him, and whatever you do, do not let your brother look in the mirror." I wouldn't let Jeremy look at himself for fear he would lose all hope. His handsome face was so disfigured that I thought he might die or be hideously ugly the rest of his life. "I've destroyed him," I thought to myself. "I spent most of my life taking care of my kids, and then in one moment I destroyed my son."

The police arrived in ten minutes. Then came an ambulance and a helicopter. After emergency workers loaded Jeremy into the helicopter and lifted him up in flight, I walked over to the tall, blond-haired stranger. He was staring across the autobahn at our car, which was demolished. "This man came at the exact moment we needed him," I began to think. "He spoke English. He had a blanket. He had a phone. He put Jeremy in his car. This is like one of those angel stories." At that very moment, the man turned to look at me and said, "Did you know you had angels protecting you tonight?"

As the police were taking down a report of the incident, they asked me, "And how did you contact us?"

"This guy who had the car. . ." I told them. "He had a cell phone with him." They looked around and asked, "What guy?" The man was gone.

"How could the police have pulled up and not seen him or his car?" I wondered. It turned out the police didn't even have a trace of his call.

I will let Jeremy tell what happened next, as it is hard for me to share the details of his ongoing suffering.

When I came out of shock, I was in a dark room in the basement of the hospital, lying on what felt like a stainless-steel table. I awoke surrounded by doctors who didn't speak English. I thought I'd been left there to die because my condition was hopeless. For fifteen hours, I lay there, fading in and out of consciousness, and every time I came to, I had to vomit up all the blood that I was swallowing. My dad didn't know where I was, and the hospital didn't yet know I had good insurance, so I wasn't receiving any care. I can recall asking the doctors, "Is my dad alive?" because I didn't remember having seen him at all. But none of them could answer me.

When my dad finally found me and convinced the staff of his excellent insurance, I was suddenly offered red-carpet care. The staff quickly wheeled away an elderly man and another sick patient from my room to make it my own suite, while a team of top medical specialists poured in. Of all the hospitals in Europe and the United States, I was in the premier hospital for facial reconstruction surgery. My face was so torn apart that I had to go in immediately for fifteen hours of surgical reparative measures. I remained in the Vienna hospital for twelve days, and then I was transferred home.

Fourteen more oral and facial surgeries followed over the next four years, as doctors gradually tried to "restore" me. My mouth had been totally split open. Facial surgeons had to sew my detached tongue back to the bottom of my mouth. Much of my jawbone was crushed and broken so they had to reconstruct my jaw line. Because my cheekbone was destroyed and my eye socket smashed, surgeons had to insert plates into my face so that all of the bones would remain intact. They had to rip off pieces from the top of my mouth to build new gums to hold my new teeth. I had a screw sticking out of my chin, just below my mouth, because I was missing parts of the bone that had held my lower teeth. With a tiny screw driver, I had to turn the screw a millimeter each day to raise the bone the tiniest hair so my chin would re-grow itself. Doctors had pulled the skin away from my eye in order to place a utensil down the inside of my face. They had cut skin away from my cheek to better see my broken bones on a screen and piece them all back together. For added flare, they put a balloon inside my cheek with a cord that came down through my nose so I could pump it up with air. If I'd wanted to be cured of vanity, now was the time.

There were moments when I wondered why God allowed things to happen as they did. I had to take a semester off from school, and during those months, I would sleep sixteen to eighteen hours a day because of the trauma to my brain and the constant pain. At least every other day for many months, I had to rouse myself to visit a doctor when my body couldn't imagine moving an inch. I knew that God never does anything by accident, that everything has a purpose, but still I had to make an act of faith many, many times: "Lord, I trust in you. I know you're going to work through this, even though I don't understand how."

Over the course of time, I came to understand clearly that the accident was one of the greatest gifts God has ever given me. To give one example, my dad was very strict when I was growing up, and I'd always felt that things had to go his way or the highway. Though I always knew he loved me, he was unable to express it verbally and struggled to show his affection for me. He could not say, "I love you."

When I was forced to spend a semester at home, essentially bedbound, except for doctor visits, I would see my dad every evening at dinner. With my mouth torn apart and swollen, I could only eat pureed food for several weeks, most of which would fall from my mouth and drop onto my bib and tray. Every evening, my mom would spoon-feed me, like she did when I was an infant, wiping off my chin and scooping up what she could. And every evening from across the table, my dad would sit, looking at me with tears welling in his eyes, sometimes wiping them from his cheeks. I began to realize that God allowed everything for the healing of our relationship because I was able to see how much my dad loved me. I know without a

150

doubt that he suffered more than I did through the accident and all that transpired afterward. I didn't understand the ordeal while I was going through it, but the aftermath was better than anything I could have imagined. Honestly, I would have endured it all just for that, just for the mending of our relationship.

I knew that God would always bring good out of suffering, but I, too, wondered for a long time what purpose there was for God allowing this terrible accident—until I really looked at Jeremy and saw his great faith, strength, fortitude, and tremendous compassion for others. Suddenly, my son was all grown up. He had to suffer mentally, spiritually, and physically with excruciating pain for months on end, and never once did he complain. The only time I saw his pain was when he looked in the mirror for the first time after the accident. Tears started to run down his face. But he never said a word, never uttered a single "I'm suffering" or "It hurts."

What was God's gift to me? I gained an appreciation for Our Lady's offering of her Son. My children mean everything to me, and no parent ever wants to lose a child. When I was sitting on that highway divider in Austria, holding Jeremy in my arms in the cold blackness of night, I was given the grace to see that good can come from anything. In what I can only describe as a state of serene agony, I felt an inner communion with Our Lady like never before or since.

I believe that Mother Mary was truly there with me then, and she has been actively with me in every critical moment of my life. She is the hidden hand that brought me and my family to her Son and his Church, the tender arms that have carried me through my darkest moments. She is the loving mother I felt unashamed to approach when sorrow and guilt kept me from turning to her Son. She is the catalyst for my family's conversion, the guiding light of their salvation, and the inspiration for my son Jeremy's conversion and his priesthood.

After my pilgrimage to Medjugorje, I felt it was Our Lady's desire that my family go there with me one day, so I prayed for this intention for many years. Again, God answered my prayer, not in the way I imagined or in the time frame I had hoped, but better than I could have dreamed. Eight years after I traveled to Medjugorje, I took Jennifer and the kids there, and we were blessed beyond measure. My children then led five more pilgrimages to Medjugorje, bringing their neighbors, friends, and families. Altogether, our family has organized over twelve pilgrimages to Medjugorje, taking groups of forty or fifty people at a time, and we've witnessed multiple conversions. As a result, my ten brothers and sisters are all back in the faith, as are their children. My wife and all of my four children are striving to be saints. I don't know where my family and I would be today without Our Lady. What began on December 22, the day my father had us baptized Catholic—a day we have celebrated with a Mass and dinner every year since—was set aflame by Medjugorje.

It astounds me how one can teach the truth, take people to church, have them read spiritual books, and little changes; but take them to Medjugorje, and they're often converted within a week. When I give people literature about Medjugorje and the messages, or I encourage them to go on a pilgrimage, their lives transform.

I am extremely happy to see now that the Church has approved official pilgrimages and supports Medjugorje gatherings and conferences. Though the commission established by Pope Benedict XVI to investigate Medjugorje were in near-unanimous agreement that the first seven days of the apparitions were real, some people still distance themselves from Medjugorje and will not travel there because they want to be faithful to the Church, which has not yet formally approved the apparitions. However, this is not a Catholic way, nor a Christian way of thinking. If this were a proper response, then there would have been no one to witness the miracle of the sun at Fatima, no one to go into the healing waters at Lourdes. The Church, as a good Mother, has given us the charge: "Do not quench the Spirit. Do not despise prophetic utterances. Test everything; retain what is good" (1 Thes 5:19-21).

I hear others say, "I can go visit the Blessed Sacrament here. The Mass contains the greatest prayer to God. I don't need to go to Medjugorje." And that is true. But for some reason, God seems to think that we need Our Blessed Mother right now because he's sending her, and I don't have a better idea than he does. I've often thought, "How did I learn about the value of the Mass? Where did I find out about Adoration? Where did I learn about my faith? Where did I learn how to pray? It was Our Lady who taught me in her school of Medjugorje.

The last to bend was my father. One thing he had no desire to do was to go to Medjugorje, even though his ten children and fifty-six grandkids were alive in the faith because of it: "I can pray to Our Lady right here. In fact, I pray to her all the time. I don't need to see miracles. I already have faith." Stubbornly resistant, he wouldn't go. Ten years after the rest of his family had first traveled there, including his wife, my dad said spontaneously, "I think I'm going to go to Medjugorje."

"I thought you didn't have to . . ."

"I don't have to. But I want to. I just want to go by myself." He wouldn't even take my mother.

When my father was in Medjugorje, he had no desire to see any miracles. He believed they were a distraction, even a detraction, from true faith; he didn't need reasons to believe or "selfish amusements." It so happened that during his pilgrimage, on the day the visionary Mirjana received her monthly apparition of the Blessed Mother, my dad was present only a few feet away from her. He watched intently as Mirjana's head suddenly tilted upward, her eyes focused a few feet above and in front of her, and her face softened with an expressive look of tenderness, awe, and love. He was so close as to see the tears running down her cheeks. Like son, like father, he was inundated by such powerful feelings that he had to get away. While Mary continued to appear to Mirjana on earth, he began walking through the grape fields. Only moments later, a man in front of him looked down at his rosary and gasped, "My rosary turned gold!"

Then another man pulled his rosary out of his pocket and exclaimed, "Mine did, too!"

Irritated by the "sideshow," my father quickened his pace to pass them, when another man put his hand on my dad's shoulder and pointed to the sky: "Look! Look up!" At the very moment when my father was running away from miracles, he was confronted with one of the most spectacular of them all—the miracle of the sun.

He found himself staring directly and comfortably at the blazing source of the earth's light and heat, which was spinning rapidly and emitting every dazzling color of the rainbow. Overcome with wonder, he felt a tsunami of emotion erupt in his heart, which brought him to his knees. Time disappeared. A transcendent love washed over him and through him, and he cried and cried and cried.

Since then, my father has had the special grace of being able to see the miracle of the sun wherever he is, whenever he chooses to. My dad used to be the most stoic, stubborn person. He struggled to show what was in his heart: his love for his family and wife. We kids knew that he loved us, but he would never hug us, touch us, or say "I love you." And now my silly dad can't hide his tender feelings and weeps all the time. When the subject of Mary or faith comes up, he can't help but cry. He's even worse than I . . . thanks to our Mother in heaven.

A NOTE TO THE READER

AMAZON REVIEWS

If you were graced by these stories, would you kindly post a short review of *Of Men and Mary* on Amazon.com? Your support will make a difference in the lives of souls and help spread the Good News.

    To leave a short review, go to Amazon.com and type in *Of Men and Mary*. Click on the book and scroll down the page. Next to customer reviews, click on "Write a customer review."

BOOK TRAILER

If you are curious to see the faces of the men you have just read about and would like to watch the trailer for this book, go to www.queenofpeacemedia.com/men.

FREE E-BOOK

There is one more story that didn't find its way into this book (only because of lack of room!) It is the eyebrow-lifting adventure of Fr. Mark Beard, a man who was married to "money, power, and dating for medicinal purposes: the unholy Trinity," until he traveled to Medjugorje only to debunk the "hubbub." For the free e-book of his story, go to www.queenofpeacemedia.com/beard.

FOR THE OF MEN AND MARY AUDIO BOOK
go to Amazon.com

APPENDIX

A BRIEF ACCOUNT OF THE MEDJUGORJE APPARITIONS

On June 24, 1981, in a remote village in the former communist Yugoslavia, two teenage girls, Mirjana and Ivanka, went for a walk. As they exchanged the latest news in their lives, Ivanka suddenly noticed a light high up on Mount Podbrdo, the large hill behind the village. Looking up, she saw a woman, radiating with light, hovering above the ground on a cloud and holding a baby in her arms. Ivanka said to Mirjana, "I think that Our Lady is on the hill." Mirjana, not bothering to glance up, responded glibly, "Yes, Our Lady has nothing better to do than to come to the two of us."

Brushing off Ivanka's strange behavior, she left and walked back toward the village, but she soon felt a great urge to return. When she did, she found Ivanka in the same spot, still staring at the hill, mesmerized. "Look at it now, please," said Ivanka. Mirjana looked up and saw a beautiful woman with blue eyes and long, dark hair, dressed in a gray dress and a white veil, with a baby in her arms and a crown of twelve stars around her head. Mirjana says of that instant, "All the possible emotions that exist I felt in my heart at the same time. To put it simply, I was not aware if I was alive or dead."

Just then, a friend of theirs named Vicka was passing by, looking for the two of them, and when she, too, saw the woman on the hill, she jumped out of her slippers and ran headlong back to the village. A few moments later, a teenage boy named Ivan walked by on his way home carrying apples in his arms, and upon seeing the woman, threw down the apples and ran away. Then Mirjana said to Ivanka, "Who knows what's going on? It's better for us to go home as well."

The next day, all four children felt drawn back to the same spot (which is now called Apparition Hill). Vicka ran to get her friend, Marija, and ten-

157

year-old Jakov, and all six children saw the beautiful woman. Then again, the following day after that, July 26, they saw her—this time with nearly the entire village present. On that day, more than five thousand people saw the visionaries bathed in an immense light and believed.

As soon as the woman appeared, Vicka, at her grandmother's urging, sprinkled holy water on her in the sign of the cross and said, "If you are Satan, go away from us." The woman just smiled with an expression of immense love, and then she spoke:

> *Do not be afraid, dear angels.*
> *I am the Mother of God.*
> *I am the Queen of Peace.*
> *I am the mother of all people.[1]*

Thus began Mary's daily apparitions to the six children, the longest-occurring series of apparitions in Church history. They continue to this day. Why has she been appearing so long? She answers this question in her message of January 25, 2009:

> *. . . I am with you for this long because you are on the wrong path. Only with my help, little children, you will open your eyes. There are many of those who, by living my messages, comprehend that they are on the way of holiness towards eternity. . . .[2]*

On the second day of the Medjugorje apparitions, Marija saw Mary crying and carrying a wooden cross. "Peace, peace, peace!" were the words she spoke. "Be reconciled! Only peace!"[3] Twenty-eight years later, in her message of April 25, 2009, she calls out to us again:

> *Dear children! Today I call you all to pray for peace and to witness it in your families so that peace may become the highest treasure on this peaceless earth. I am your Queen of Peace and your mother. I desire to lead you on the way of peace, which comes only from God. Therefore, pray, pray, pray. Thank you for having responded to my call.[4]*

Mary is appearing to a world intent on destroying itself in order to urge her children to return to the ways of God. To show to the world that her presence and words are true and real, Our Lady has promised that when she stops appearing, a visible and lasting sign, undeniably of God, will be left on the spot of her first apparition.

Mary has chosen to appear in Medjugorje and to give the world messages in order to continue the work she set out to do when she appeared to three young children in Fatima, Portugal, in 1917. Part of her message from August 25, 1991, states:

Dear Children! Today also I invite you to prayer, now as never before when my plan has begun to be realized. Satan is strong and wants to sweep away my plans of peace and joy and make you think that my Son is not strong in his decisions. Therefore, I call all of you, dear children, to pray and fast still more firmly. I invite you to self-renunciation for nine days so that, with your help, everything that I desire to realize through the secrets I began in Fatima, may be fulfilled. I call you, dear children, to now grasp the importance of my coming and the seriousness of the situation. I want to save all souls and present them to God. Therefore, let us pray that everything I have begun be fully realized. Thank you for having responded to my call. [5]

In the Church-approved apparitions at Fatima, Mary gave the three young seers three secrets; in an earlier approved apparition in La Salette, France, in 1846, she gave two young seers two secrets. These have all since been revealed. The Blessed Mother is now in the process of giving ten secrets to each of the six visionaries in Medjugorje, some of whom have received all ten. The secrets will be revealed in the not-too-distant future, as the visionary Mirjana has been asked by Mary to help publicize them through a priest at the appointed time. Mary and the visionaries tell us, however, not to focus on the secrets; only to focus on our own personal conversion, here and now.

In December 1982, a nine-year-old girl in Medjugorje, Jelena Vasilj, began to hear Our Lady speak to her interiorly, and the same gift was given to Marijana Vasilj (no relation) in March of 1983. Our Lady told them she wanted them to form a prayer group for the youth at St. James Church and spoke of her desire that all of her children be part of a prayer group. In a message to Jelena on February 25, 1985, she instructed:

Dear children, this is my advice. I would like to conquer some fault each day.

If your fault is to get angry at everything, try each day to get angry less.

If your fault is not to be able to study, try to study.

If your fault is not to be able to obey, or if you cannot stand those who do not please you, try on a given day to speak with them.

If your fault is not to be able to stand an arrogant person, you should try to approach that person.

If you desire that person to be humble, be humble yourselves. Show that humility is worth more than pride.

Each day, try to go beyond, and to reject every vice from your heart.

Find out which are the vices that you most need to reject.

Try truly to desire to spend your life in real love. Strive as much as possible. [6]

Mary is strongly urging everyone to "pray, pray, pray," and she has given five specific means to holiness that she wishes of us, in order to truly live her messages: frequent attendance of the Holy Mass, monthly Confession, Bible reading, daily prayer (especially the rosary), and fasting on bread and water on Wednesdays and Fridays—all done with the heart. "I am not God," she said in her message in December 1983, "I need your prayers and sacrifices to help me." [7] And "you have forgotten that with prayer and fasting you can ward off wars, suspend natural laws." [8]

In many of Mary's messages, she encourages us to live in joy. On June 6, 1986, she said:

Dear children, these days the Lord is allowing me to intercede for more graces for you. Thus I urge you once more to pray, dear children. Pray without ceasing. That way I can give you the joy which the Lord has given me. With these graces, dear children, your sufferings can be turned to joy. I am your mother and I want to help you. [9]

Since the apparitions began, the visionaries, who humbly say that they are not important and no more holy than you or me, spend as many as six hours or more daily in prayer and fast on bread and water up to three times a week. Following their initial fright, the six young visionaries quickly lost their fear of the Virgin Mary. They say her love for them and all of humanity cannot be expressed in words, and that to be in her presence is like being in heaven. They speak of her as "beautiful beyond anything in this world."[10] In the early days of the apparitions, they once asked her, "Why are you so beautiful?" and she responded, "I am beautiful because I love. You, too, are beautiful when you love."[11]

Tens of millions of pilgrims from all over the world have been to Medjugorje, including hundreds of bishops, dozens of archbishops, a handful of cardinals, and many thousands of priests who have publicly visited Medjugorje.[12] This does not include all of the clerics who have chosen to go privately for their own personal pilgrimage.[13] Each day, villagers and pilgrims pray for hours in the local church, while others wait in the long lines for Confession. All day, and often into the night, pilgrims climb Apparition Hill, where Mary first appeared to the children, lending their prayers to the sacred atmosphere. Nearby, pilgrims also climb Cross Mountain, upon which the villagers erected by hand a fifteen-ton, thirty-six-foot-high cross in 1933 to commemorate the 1900th anniversary of the crucifixion. Mary told the children that she chose to appear in Medjugorje because of the strong faith she found in the village, and she continues to call people from across the globe to make a pilgrimage there to encounter her Son in a special way. Those who heed her call with an open spirit find themselves in a place of extraordinary peace, where rosaries turn gold, the sun dances and spins in the sky, and miracles, conversions, and healings abound—most importantly, the healing of the human heart.

Notes

1. Story compiled from Janice Connell's *The Visions of the Children* (New York: St. Martin's Griffin, 1997), 10; *Medjugorje Magazine*, May 2002 Special issue, 14; and a videotape of Mirjana telling her story to pilgrims in December 2001, provided by Fiat Voluntas Tua.
2. www.medjugorje.org/msg09.htm.
3. Richard Beyer, *Medjugorje Day by Day* (Notre Dame, IN: Ave Maria Press, 1993), 6.
4. www.medjugorje.org/msg09.htm.
5. Mary's message of August 25, 1991. Sister Emmanuel, *Medjugorje, the '90s* (Santa Barbara, CA: Queenship Publishing Co., 1997), 69.
6. Janice Connell, *The Visions of the Children* (New York: St. Martin's Griffin, 1997), 178.
7. Beyer, *Medjugorje Day by Day,* July 14 meditation.
8. Wayne Weible, *Medjugorje the Message* (Brewster, MA: Paraclete Press, 1989), 44.

9. Beyer, *Medjugorje Day by Day,* July 27 meditation.

10. Ibid., 5.

11. Mirjana's story as told by her, captured on videotape to pilgrims in December 2001, provided by Fiat Voluntas Tua.

12. Miravalle and Weible, *Are the Medjugorje Apparitions Authentic?* back cover.

13. Denis Nolan, *Medjugorje and the Church*, 4th edition (Goleta, CA: Queenship Publishing, 2007), 36-45.

THE CATHOLIC CHURCH'S STANCE ON MEDJUGORJE

For many years, the official stance on Medjugorje by the Church came from statements made by the 1993 committee of Bishops in Zadar, Yugoslavia, organized by St. Pope John Paul II: *"We bishops, after a three-year-long commission study, accept Medjugorje as a holy place, as a shrine. This means that we have nothing against it if someone venerates the Mother of God in a manner also in agreement with the teaching and belief of the Church. . . Therefore, we are leaving that to further study. The Church does not hurry."*[2] In 1991, the same conference, had assigned one of these three official categories to the alleged apparitions: 1) *constat de supernaturalitate* (the apparition is established as supernatural), 2) *constat de non supernaturalitate* (the apparition is clearly not miraculous or lacks sufficient signs of the miraculous); or 3) *non constat de supernaturalitate* (It may not be evident whether or not the alleged apparition is authentic). The commission chose this third, in between category, neither condemning Medjugorje, nor giving final approval, since the Church almost never pronounces an apparition as authentic while it is continuing to occur.

Ignoring the official stance of the Church, the Bishop of Mostar (the diocese to which the parish belonged), Bishop Zanic, made his personal and hostile opinions of Medjugorje known, as did his successor, Bishop Ratko Peric, causing much confusion. The negative stance adopted by both Ordinaries was rendered moot when the Holy See, during the pontificate of John Paul II, consequently removed evaluation of the phenomenon from their jurisdiction: an unprecedented action the Church.

During the pontificate of Benedict XVI, there was another unprecedented move when the Vatican adopted direct jurisdiction over Medjugorje. A commission was appointed to assess the apparitions under

---

[2] (Glas Koncila, August 15, 1993).

Cardinal Ruini. Remarkably, the Ruini Commission, which met from March 2010 to January 2014, concluded in 2017, by near-unanimous agreement, that the first seven apparitions were authentic. This was an exceptional breakthrough in terms of official recognition of an apparition. Although Pope Francis has yet to officially release the Ruini report, the Pontiff, himself, confirmed in an interview that the Commission had reached this conclusion. In point of fact, the Pope had actually stopped attempts by the then Prefect of the Congregation of the Doctrine of the Faith, Cardinal Müller, to block this judgment. The pope also asked that the Ruini report be sent to him for a review and determination, as opposed to Müller, who was originally set to receive it.

On February 11, 2017, Pope Francis appointed Archbishop Henryk Hoser of Poland as his papal envoy to coordinate all matters relating to Medjugorje. In December of 2017, Archbishop Hoser shared the breaking news that the Vatican now permits official pilgrimages to Medjugorje. "Today, dioceses and other institutions can organize official pilgrimages. It's no longer a problem," he said.[3] At a recorded Medjugorje press conference on April 5, 2017, the archbishop reconfirmed this fact.[4] Müller's 2013 CDF statement that Catholics should not participate in any meetings in which the authenticity of the Medjugorje apparitions were taken for granted is now null and void. In Archbishop Hoser's own words: "My mission was not to close Medjugorje, but to evaluate whether the pastoral ministry was proper, consistent with the doctrine and teaching of the Church, effective and well organized. I conclude that this is the

---

[3] Jesús Colina, "Official pilgrimages to Medjugorje are being authorized, confirms Pope Francis' envoy," Aletia, December 7, 2017, accessed July 14, 2018, https://aleteia.org/2017/12/07/official-pilgrimages-to-medjugorje-are-being-authorized-confirms-pope-francis-envoy/.

[4] Papal envoy, Archbishop Henryk Hoser Press Conference, April 5th, 2017, streamed live through MaryTV.tv and available for viewing at http://marytv.tv/daily-rosary-3-3/. MaryTV.tv. is a Medjugorje Internet TV channel that broadcasts 24/7 to help people stay connected to important ongoing events. Free apps are available for smart phones and Apple TV. Transcription of the press conference in Polish: "Konferencija za medije posebnog izaslanika mons. Henryka Hosera," Medjugorje: Mjesto Molitve I Pomirenja, April 4, 2017, accessed July 14, 2018, http://medjugorje.hr/hr/novosti/obavijesti/konferencija-za-medije-posebnog-izaslanika-mons.-henryka-hosera,8795.html.

case. On the pastoral side my assessment is very positive. Thus, the ongoing pastoral activities, liturgical order and conferences should continue."[5]

At the conclusion of the press conference, in which he urged everyone to bring the light of Medjugorje "to the world that is sinking into darkness. . .," he stated, "You, my dear friends, should be the carriers of the joyful news. Say to the whole world that in Medjugorje we can find the light again!"[6]

It can safely be said that Medjugorje now has received as much official recognition as it can receive, given that the phenomenon is still going on. It is well known that two of the most illustrious saints of recent times, St. Mother Theresa of Calcutta and St. Pope John Paul II, were ardent devotees of the Queen of Peace of Medjugorje. Thanks to them and millions of the faithful, Medjugorje's message of repentance, reconciliation, peace, and penance has spread across the globe.

St. Pope John Paul II, when addressing American bishops at the Philadelphia Eucharistic Congress five years before Our Lady's apparitions in Medjugorje began, stated:

We are now standing in the face of the greatest historical confrontation humanity has ever experienced. . . We are now facing the final confrontation between the Church and the anti-church, between the Gospel and the anti-gospel, between Christ and the antichrist. This confrontation lies within the plans of Divine Providence. It is therefore in God's plan and a trial which the Church must take up!

Given that St. John Paul II understood that these days were those of the final confrontation, when he learned of Our Lady's coming to Medjugorje and her words, "I have descended among you," he knew her presence with us had now changed everything. To Monsignor Murilo

[5] "Breaking News—Historic Moment in Catholic Church History...Vatican Special Envoy to Medjugorje: 'Everything indicates that the apparitions will be recognized, perhaps even this year.'" Published at Deon.pl (Catholic News Site in Poland—8.18.2017), August 18, 2017, accessed July 14, 2018, https://mysticpost.com/2017/08/breaking-news-historic-moment-catholic-church-history-making-vatican-special-envoy-medjugorje-everything-indicates-apparitions-will-recognized-perhaps-even-year/.
[6] Ibid., Papal envoy, Archbishop Henryk Hoser Press Conference

Sebastiao Ramos Krieger, Archbishop of Florianopolis in Brazil, he stated, "Medjugorje is the spiritual center of the world!" He told friends, including Cardinal Frantisek Tomasek, who made the words public, that if he weren't Pope, he'd be living in Medjugorje as a priest, helping to hear confessions. In the Pope's own hand, he wrote to friends in Poland:

I thank Sophia for everything concerning Medjugorje. I too go there every day as a pilgrim in my prayers. I unite in my prayers with all those who pray there or receive a call for prayer from there. Today we have understood this call better. I rejoice that our time is not lacking people of prayer and apostles.

St. Pope John Paul II fully believed and told us in his will that "Victory when it comes, will be a victory through Maria!"

Dear children, my real living presence among you should make you happy because this is the great love of my Son. He is sending me among you so that, with a motherly love, I may grant you safety!

—Medjugorje message from Our Lady on July 2, 2016

Denis Nolan
MaryTV.tv
Author of *Medjugorje and the Church*

THE MEDJUGORJE TESTAMENT OF FR. RENÉ LAURENTIN (1917-2017)

Fr. René Laurentin, one of the world's leading experts in Mariology, was among the many important figures in the Church who grasped the urgency and supreme importance of Mary's presence in Medjugorje at this time in the world's history. Trained in classical theology, he was not inclined toward apparitions: "I did not search them out, they came and looked for me." His success in the research and extensive writings on apparitions asked of him, he became, in spite of himself, a specialist in the subject. As a prolific author, a renowned professor, a consummate researcher and scholar, and recipient of numerous awards in the Church, his knowledge is profound and his words are a poignant reminder of the need for our world to wake up to the grace that is being given to us now, and not to waste it in hostility, indifference, doubt or delay:

TESTAMENT

This being my time of testament, I present here not my last will, for I have no other will but God's and the Church's. This will is not always easy to clarify, but much hope is placed on the Lord. . .

Do not close your eyes to the flow of grace, which is without equal in the Church today, at least as pertains to the conversions, and the confessions, and the healings for which many give thanks to God. . .

You who tolerate and support so many institutions where prayer is disappearing, where faith and sometimes morals are disintegrating, where vocations are few or are lost, do not fight against this unequalled source of conversions and vocations. . .

167

You who, according to the doctrines of the Church and of the Bible, are respectful of life in all its forms, and discourage abortions, do not perpetrate abortion of this great grace. . .

Do not dissuade the pilgrimages which have borne so many conversions and spiritual discoveries for the service of the Church. Do not uproot this garden of graces which has played such a providential role in the present conflict in the Church and against the invasion of sects. . .

Do not perpetuate the obstinacy of the scribes and Pharisees about which the Gospel of the man born blind gives such a clear lesson. . .[7]

---

[7] Fr. René Laurentin, Medjugorje Testament: Hostility Abounds, Grace Superabounds (The Latest News #17) (Toronto, Ontario: Ave Maria Press, 1998), 175-176.

MESSAGES AND PILGRIMAGES

If you would like to read the messages that Mary is giving the world through Medjugorje on the 2nd and 25th of each month, go to www.medjugorjemiracles.com. The messages are also posted on the Queen of Peace Media Facebook page: www.facebook.com/QueenofPeaceMedia. Click "Like" to receive them.

For information on pilgrimages to Medjugorje, hosted by the visionary Mirjana Dragicevic-Soldo, contact:

Trinity Pilgrimages
Jim Benzow, Managing Director
8742 E. Via Taz Norte
Scottsdale, AZ 85258
(480) 443-3912
(602) 319-5289

trinitypilgrimage@cox.net

www.trinitypilgrimage.com

OTHER BOOKS

BY THE AUTHOR

Available in Print, E-book & Audio Book Formats
at QueenofPeaceMedia.com and Amazon.com
Go to:
www.queenofpeacemedia.com/catholic-bookstore

MARY'S MANTLE CONSECRATION

A SPIRITUAL RETREAT FOR HEAVEN'S HELP

Also available in Spanish—*El Manto de María: Una Consagración Mariana para Ayuda Celestial*

Endorsed by **Archbishop Salvatore Cordilcone** and **Bishop Myron J. Cotta**

(See www.MarysMantleConsecration.com to see a video of amazing testimonies and to order)

"I am grateful to Christine Watkins for making this disarmingly simple practice, which first grew in the fertile soil of Mexican piety, available to the English-speaking world."

—**Archbishiop Salvatore Cordileone**

"Now more than ever, we need a miracle. Christine Watkins leads us through a 46-day self-guided retreat that focuses on daily praying of the Rosary, a Little fasting, and meditating on various virtues and the seven gifts of the Holy Spirit, leading to a transformation in our lives and in the people on the journey with us!"

—**Fr. Sean O. Sheridan, TOR**
President, Franciscan University of Steubenville

171

MARY'S MANTLE CONSECRATION

PRAYER JOURNAL
to accompany the consecration book

Also available in Spanish—
El Manto de Maria: Diario de Oración para la Consagración

PREPARE FOR AN OUTPOURING
OF GRACE UPON YOUR LIFE

(See www.MarysMantleConsecration.com
to see a video of amazing testimonies and to order)

St. Pope John Paul II said that his consecration to Mary was "a decisive turning point in my life." It can be the same for you.

This *Prayer Journal* with daily Scriptures, saint quotes, questions for reflection and space for journaling is a companion book to the popular *Mary's Mantle Consecration*, a self-guided retreat that has resulted in miracles in the lives and hearts of those who have applied themselves to it. This prayer journal will take you even deeper into your soul and into God's transforming grace.

172

FULL OF GRACE

MIRACULOUS STORIES OF HEALING AND CONVERSION THROUGH MARY'S INTERCESSION

"Christine Watkins's beautiful and touching collection of conversion stories are direct, honest, heart-rending, and miraculous."

BEST-SELLER

—**Wayne Weible**
Author of *Medjugorje: The Message*

(See www.queenofpeacemedia.com/full-of-grace for the book trailer and to order)

In this riveting book, Christine Watkins tells her dramatic story of miraculous healing and conversion to Catholicism, along with the stories of five others: a homeless drug addict, an altar boy trapped by cocaine, a stripper, a lonely youth, and a modern-day hero.

Following each story is a message that Mary has given to the world. And for those eager to probe the deeper, reflective waters of discipleship—either alone or within a prayer group—a Scripture passage, prayerful reflection questions, and a spiritual exercise at the end of each chapter offer an opportunity to enliven our faith.

TRANSFIGURED

PATRICIA SANDOVAL'S ESCAPE FROM DRUGS, HOMELESSNESS, AND THE BACK DOORS OF PLANNED PARENTHOOD

Endorsed by
Archbishop Salvatore Cordileone & Bishop Michael C. Barber, SJ

Also available in Spanish: *TRANSFIGURADA*
(See www.queenofpeacemedia.com/transfigured
for the book trailer, the companion DVD, and to order)

"Are you ready to read one of the most powerful conversion stories ever written? Seriously, are you? It's a bold and shocking claim, I admit. But the story you are about to have the pleasure of reading is so intense and brutally candid that I wouldn't be surprised if it brings you to tears multiple times and opens the door to an experience of mercy and healing. This story is made for the big screen, and I pray it makes it there someday. It's that incredible.

. . . What you are about to read is as raw, real, and riveting as a story can get. I couldn't put this book down!"

—Fr. Donald Calloway, MIC
Author of *No Turning Back*

174

THE WARNING

TESTIMONIES AND PROPHECIES OF THE ILLUMINATION OF CONSCIENCE

Includes the riveting story of Marino Restrepo, hailed as a St. Paul for our century

(See www.queenofpeacemedia.com/the-warning for the book trailer and to order)

"Christine Watkins' *The Warning* should be widely read and discerned seriously with an open mind." **—Dr. Mark Miravalle, STD**
Chair of Mariology, Franciscan University of Steubenville

Authentic accounts of saints and mystics of the Church who have spoken of a day when we will all see our souls in the light of truth, and fascinating stories of those who have already experienced it for themselves.

"With His divine love, He will open the doors of hearts and illuminate all consciences. Every person will see himself in the burning fire of divine truth. It will be like a judgment in miniature."
—Our Lady to Fr. Stefano Gobbi
Marian Movement of Priests

175

ABOUT THE AUTHOR

Christine Watkins is a popular Catholic author and keynote speaker. She was an anti-Catholic atheist about to die from her sins when she received a divine healing. Watkins brings to life stories of faith, including her own, and fascinating topics of Catholic spirituality.

See www.ChristineWatkins.com.

FIND YOUR WAY HOME

A special talk or retreat for our turbulent times that
reenergizes excitement about the faith and makes true disciples

See www.ChristineWatkins.com

For more information email cwatkins@queenofpeacemedia.com

Made in the USA
Monee, IL
06 March 2020